Robert E. Webber

WORSHIP IS A Verb

WORD BOOKS
PUBLISHER
WACO, TEXAS
A DIVISION OF
WORD, INCORPORATED

WORSHIP IS A VERB

Library of Congress Cataloging in Publication Data:

Webber, Robert.
    Worship is a verb.

    1. Public worship. I. Title.
BV15.W39 1985   264   84–25720
ISBN 0-8499-0371-8
ISBN 0-8499-3089-8 (paperback)

Printed in the United States of America

7 8 9 8 FG 9 8 7 6 5 4 3 2 1

*Dedicated
to my friends
at Bethany Beach*

CONTENTS

During the past few years a number of books on the subject of worship have been published by evangelical publishing companies. Since public worship has been a neglected subject among Evangelicals for decades, the publication of these books has contributed greatly to the quest for worship renewal among us.

So, you ask, why another book on worship?

This is a question I also had to confront when *Worship Is a Verb* was in the planning stage. As a result of my struggle to come up with an answer, I have written a book that I think is uniquely different from other books currently on the market, including my own *Worship Old and New.*

Worship Is a Verb has grown out of workshops I have led on worship. These workshops are designed to help a congregation evaluate the worship of their church, step by step, and plan a specific program of worship renewal that meets the needs of their particular church.

What makes *Worship Is a Verb* unique is that it's a course of programmed study. Chapter one introduces four principles of worship that are applicable to any congregation. The eight chapters that follow alternately discuss each principle in detail and offer practical ways to apply the principle to worship. For example, in chapter two I describe how worship is meant to celebrate the events in Christ's life. Then, in chapter three, I present an order for worship which is based on these events. This pattern—principle and application—continues throughout the remaining chapters of the book. Finally, the study guide at the end can be used by an entire congregation or by small groups within a church community as a means of putting the whole concept into perspective.

I envision groups of people using the book primarily as a study guide and tool for the implementation of worship renewal. Although it will have particular value for the pastoral staff, the worship committee, a Sunday school class, or other study groups within the church, the book is also written in such a way that interested persons may simply read it without pursuing a study of the subject.

In an attempt to orient this material to a worshiping community and design it for use by lay people, I interviewed a number of pastors and church workers who are involved in worship renewal in their local churches. I wish to thank these people for their insights and help.

My particular thanks go to the Reverend Ames Broen, pastor of the Mayfair Presbyterian Church in Chicago; Professor James Young, director of theatre at Wheaton College; Reverend Henry Jauhiainen, pastor of the Crystal Valley Church in Crystal Lake, Illinois; Professor Joel Sheesley, professor of art at Wheaton College; Professor Alva Steffler, professor of art at Wheaton College; Reverend Loren McLean, pastor of the Geneva Road Baptist Church in Wheaton, Illinois; Reverend David Mains, former pastor of Circle Church in Chicago and now director and pastor of Chapel of the Air in Wheaton, Illinois; Professor Mary Hopper, professor of music at the Wheaton College Conservatory; the Reverend William Mahlow, pastor of the Church of the Good Shepherd in Valparaiso, Indiana; Peter Robb, musician and former lay worship leader at the Open Door Fellowship Church, Phoenix, Arizona; Dr. Dan Sharp, music minister of Grace Chapel, Lexington, Massachusetts; and Robert Harvey, pastor of Bethel Presbyterian Church, Wheaton, Illinois. I wish also to express a special thanks to my editors, Floyd Thatcher and Kathleen Mohr, at Word Books. Their interest in helping me write to the lay person has been of inestimable value to me. Finally, a word of thanks goes to Mary Lou McCurdy and Jane Marston, secretaries of the Bible and Religion Department at Wheaton College, who have faithfully typed and corrected the manuscript.

CHAPTER ONE

Winds of Change

Vic Gordon and I were sitting in a booth at the brightly lighted Wheaton Restaurant, a favorite haunt of faculty and students of Wheaton College. Vic smiled as he ordered his breakfast. And so he should. After all, he was only thirty-one years old and had just been appointed chaplain of the college.

He leaned toward me, and with an eager sense of anticipation in his eyes, he said, "Bob, we've got to do some worship in chapel. I mean something different than the ordinary hymn, prayer, sermon, and prayer sequence." He was talking to the right person because that's exactly how I feel about college chapel and the Sunday morning service of the average church—both are too much like another classroom monologue. He continued, "I want you to take two chapels this fall. Speak on worship in the first service and lead us in worship in the second one."

When the day came for me to speak in chapel, I began by emphasizing the need to rediscover the focus of worship. "The focus of worship," I said, "is not human experience, not a lecture, not entertainment, but Jesus Christ—his life, death, and resurrection."

Several students in the back shouted, "Amen," which

is almost unprecedented at Wheaton. I stopped my sermon and spoke directly to the "Ameners." "I like it when you respond," I said. "One of the problems of evangelical worship is the passive nature of the congregation. We just sit and never do anything except sing a hymn or two and put money in the plate." To this statement a whole slew of "Amens" resounded. The rest of my short talk was punctuated by interactive remarks which made me realize that more students than I would have guessed felt the need to break through passive worship and become more active and involved.

What happened in chapel that day exemplifies what is happening in the larger evangelical community. Such an occurrence suggests to me that we may well be part of an exciting change—a change from passive worship to active worship. I hope this book helps this transition along and provides a guide that will lead a congregation into an active and more fulfilling worship. In other words, WORSHIP IS A VERB. It is not something done to us or for us, but by us.

In order for worship to become a verb, I am not suggesting that we deny either our convictions or roots. Rather, I am suggesting that we consider restoring some essentially evangelical practices in worship which, when regained, will restore an active quality to our worship. In no way am I suggesting the use of faddish, innovative gimmicks. Rather, it seems to me that active worship can and will be restored as the Holy Spirit opens before us certain biblical and early church insights and practices.

It was about ten to fifteen years ago that I first became aware of my need for a deeper worship experience. I was no longer satisfied to sit passively in the Sunday morning service. I wanted to be more involved, to be more than a mere observer, to do something more than watch and listen. I felt the need to participate—to see, hear, feel, taste, smell, and move as I worshiped the Lord.

This growing feeling of inner dissatisfaction caused me

to reflect on my feelings. And after some pondering, I was able to identify four things that were disturbing me about so many of our worship services.

First, *I began to see that much of our worship is dominated by the pastor.* From early childhood, I have been accustomed to the pastor doing everything. But in the past few years, I've noticed that I have become particularly sensitive to pastor-dominated worship services. Whenever I worship or speak at a church where the pastor is the focal point, I feel dominated and stifled. I find myself longing to participate, to be involved. I want to respond to what's going on, to say "Amen" or "Thanks be to God" or give witness to my faith or pray. But in churches where the pastor-figure is central, any response is often looked at as odd or inappropriate. In this situation my stomach actually feels tied up in knots, my muscles tense, and my whole body feels trapped, even caged in. My spirit and thus my worship is affected. I feel as though I'm not worshiping; I'm not actively participating. Rather, the pastor is doing everything for me. I'm simply a receiver, a passive recipient of the actions of one other person.

Second, *I began to feel that the congregation was little more than an audience.* It is true we live in an "audience society." We sit passively and are entertained by television or radio or stereo. As spectators, we listen and watch, but we seldom participate actively.

This same mood is often carried over into our church services. We simply transfer what we do at home in front of the TV set to what we do in church and let the pastor become our entertainer.

In my conversations with pastors I've found a growing awareness of this problem. Pastor Loren McLean of Geneva Road Baptist Church in Wheaton said, "I feel like I'm producing a program for people to come and watch." Layman Jim Young, director of theatre at Wheaton College expressed the frustration many pastors must feel when he said, "You've got to wow the audience." This lays a heavy burden on the pastor to perform rather than lead the congregation in worship.

I think there is another problem related to an audience mentality. It seems that many of our services shift from true worship to what Henry Jauhiainen, pastor of the Crystal Valley Church in Crystal Lake, Illinois, refers to as serving "up the secrets of the good life." With all the complexities of our world today, the temptation to turn worship into a giant psychiatric couch or a pep rally for human potential is great. I agree with Pastor Jauhiainen when he says, "I don't know of anything that could hinder proper corporate worship more than that." Christian pep rallies and success services may fulfill the needs of some, but a congregation that wants to be led in worship is not an audience to be entertained by persuasive speeches or show business gimmicks.

Third, *I began to sense that "free worship" is not necessarily free.* I have a great deal of respect for the tradition of "free worship." Originally, it was a reaction against cold, dead, and fixed liturgical forms. The intention of its proponents was to introduce congregational participation and involvement into the church and create an atmosphere which was conducive to an inner and spontaneous response to God in worship. But I feel that somehow the pendulum has swung to the other extreme. In many of our churches, what was once free has now become a fixed form with little life and spontaneity.

I agree with Peter Robb, an active layman and former worship director in the Open Door Fellowship Church of Phoenix. He says, "There is a myth that if [worship] is spontaneous, it is more holy than if it were planned." I've worshiped in Plymouth Brethren churches where the people wait on the Spirit of God to lead their worship. In these churches I have always found more planning (in the sense of an order of worship that tells a story) than I have in the average evangelical church. They seem to follow the sequence of Preparation, comments on the

Word, celebration of the Communion Table, and Dismissal in a very thoughtful way. In the worship of Plymouth Brethren churches I'm carried into the presence of God. I hear him speak, I respond to him, I commune with him at his Table, and I'm sent forth.

In some evangelical churches, there is little sense of a deliberately planned sequence. I sometimes get the feeling that hymns, prayers, Scripture, and testimony are simply thrown together without much thought about anything other than the need to have something to do to get to the main reason for being in church—the sermon. The service might start with a dismissal hymn like "Onward Christian Soldiers" and end with a preparation hymn like "Holy, Holy, Holy." Prayer, which should be a response to God's Word, will often come before the reading of the Scripture. It's surprising to note how often services include very little Scripture.

I also think lack of planning contributes to the dull and sterile sense of sameness that characterizes so many of our services Sunday after Sunday. Many evangelical churches do virtually the same thing in Advent that they do in Lent or during Epiphany or in the Easter season. So, there is little variety, other than that provided by the changing secular calendar, not only in the week-to-week Sunday service, but also throughout the church year.

I believe that this almost hypnotic sameness and dedication to a particular brand of "free form" worship is robbing us of a richness in worship that is desperately needed. As I reflected on my needs, I realized that I desired an order of worship through which God is working to communicate his message of saving grace. I need to experience and participate personally in the biblical events as God reaches down to me and in worship brings me the benefit of what he did for me through his Son on the cross. Then, I am quickened spiritually and made alive through worship.

Fourth, *for me, the mystery was gone.* I can remember

times in my life when I've experienced the mystery—
the awe and reverence—of the woods, or of the desert,
or of a snow-capped mountain far above the timber line,
a sense of the creation "telling the glory of God" (Ps.
19:1). But, unfortunately, we so seldom experience awe
and reverence in our churches. All too often the atmosphere seems to work against reverence. Our churches
are characterized by a feeling of over-familiarity, an inap-
propriateness in the approach to God. The sense of transcendence and the otherness and holiness of God seems
to be missing. A kind of secularization has taken place.

One very obvious form of secularization may be found
in most evangelical church calendars. We are organized
around the academic calendar, the seasonal calendar, the
national calendar, and the secular calendar of special
days. We celebrate Mother's Day, the Fourth of July,
Memorial Day, and the like. But when it comes to the
sacred seasons of Advent, Christmas, Epiphany, Lent,
Holy Week, Easter, and Pentecost, we have reduced our
celebrations to Christmas Sunday, Good Friday, and
Easter. We don't seem to have that sense of spiritual
time—a sense of the mystery of Christ's life, death, and
resurrection, unfolding in time throughout the year. However, I'm beginning to sense a change. More and more
pastors feel what Neil Garrabrant, pastor of the Countryside Chapel in Glen Ellyn, Illinois, expressed to me: "One
weakness I've sensed in my approach to worship is that
I have given very little consideration to the church year."
Personally, in both corporate and personal worship, I
have found the church year to be a guide to my spiritual
life.

Another way in which secularization has permeated
the church is in our music. Many of our contemporary
popular songs are not directed to God, nor do they glory
in the cross of Christ. Rather, they concentrate on personal experience and self-realization. They participate in
the narcissism of our culture, in what writer Tom Wolfe

has called the "me-generation." Our religion has followed the curvature of a self-centered culture.

Dan Sharp, the music and worship minister at Grace Chapel in Lexington, Massachusetts, feels that much contemporary Christian music feeds into this self-centered mentality. "In music," he says, "anything that is cutesy, where you notice the cleverness of the music more than the message that is being communicated, is inappropriate."

The mystery also seems to be gone from the Communion Table. Many of my students express bewilderment about the bread and wine. What does it mean? What is supposed to happen? How am I to feel? All these questions unveil a failure to grasp the transcendent nature of this sign.

In fact, we pay little attention to how God communicates to us through signs and symbols that reach down into the very depths of our being and touch us where words cannot go. As we have worshiped at the altar of "realism," we have reduced human persons to a thing—a mind—and have neglected the power of our God-given imaginations and the role of the senses as vehicles through which God can communicate to us and we with him.

FIVE NEW INSIGHTS

As I wrestled with the four concerns we've just looked at, there were times when I thought I couldn't make it through another service. However, even while I was reacting negatively, new insights and a fresh approach to worship were beginning to take shape in my thinking.

First, *I began to see that the primary work of the church is worship.* I grew up on the fundamentalist side of the evangelical tradition. For as long as I can remember, it was impressed upon me that the most important part of being a Christian was being a witness. For example, as a nine-year-old boy, I attended Camp Shadowbrook in the Pocono Mountains of Pennsylvania, which was sponsored by Percy Crawford. There I became so inspired by my calling to be a soul winner that, after camp, I went home and for a week or two I spent part of every day going door to door witnessing. Later, as a college student, I was told again that my single calling in life was to be a soul winner. It was all right if we Christians were called to be doctors, lawyers, and teachers, as long as we were soul winners first.

Evangelism is an exceedingly important work of the church as is teaching, fellowship, servanthood, missions, and the healing of broken lives. But it is worship, I gradually discovered, that really stands behind all these activities. The church is first a worshiping community. Evangelism and other functions of ministry flow from the worship of the church.

I found general agreement with this insight among those pastors and lay people I interviewed for this book. Layman Peter Robb said, "Worship should be the central activity of the church." Pastor Loren McLean feels that "the worship service is the key barometer of where the church is." David Mains, pastor of the Chapel of the Air in Wheaton and former pastor of Circle Church in Chicago, said, "There is an overwhelming hunger for God. The current concern for worship derives from that deeper sense of hunger." And Dan Sharp said, "I want people to leave the Sunday service with a conscious awareness of God." Indeed, I have discovered in my own life that corporate worship is the taproot of my life. It is the source of my spiritual life and growth.

Second, *I rediscovered that worship is a source for spiritual renewal.* In my background I always saw worship in terms of evangelism or education. The sermon was, in my mind, the central thing. That's why I went to church. But the sermon's affect on me depended on its *intent.* Sometimes the sermon would be geared toward the unsaved. On those occasions I felt it was meant for somebody else and not for me. On other occasions the sermons were educational in content. I felt like I was back in school, being lectured to again.

More recently, however, I have discovered a whole new dimension in worship. I have experienced what I call "worship from above." In worship God is speaking and acting, bringing to me the benefits of redemption. Through worship, God works on my behalf. He repairs and renews my relationship with him. Just as he has always sought people out to bring them to himself, so he now seeks me out in worship to bring healing into my life.

Consequently, worship for me is no longer something I do because of social or peer pressure. It's not a requirement that I endure for legalistic reasons, or a painful process in which my sensitivities are offended. Rather, worship is an experience I long to have, a necessary part of my spiritual diet, a central source of my spiritual formation.

I have come to see that, in reality, worship is a celebration. It is the celebration of the event of Christ—his death and resurrection. To celebrate Christ, not my devotion to him, frees me from having to create or invent my worship. Both preaching and the Lord's Supper celebrate Christ and through them Christ is given to me. Consequently, I am spiritually nourished by what God is doing for me through the Scriptures and the Communion Table.

Third, *worship became an active experience for me.* When I began to experience God at work in worship, speaking to me and moving toward me through the symbols and the preaching, I broke through the passivity which I had previously known and responded.

I learned that the God who spoke, speaks. He who spoke in times past through the prophets and apostles was now speaking to me through them. Scripture reading in worship is no mere recital of past events. Rather, it is part of the immediate experience of God bringing the power and effect of that passage into my present experience and applying it to my life.

Scripture that is imbued with this kind of power cannot be passively received. It deserves a response, a hearty "Thanks be to God," a statement of faith affirmation, a sharing of its power in my life.

I also learned that the God who acted, acts. In worship God is present, loving me, caring for me, bringing me to himself, and offering me the benefits of his work on my behalf. How can I not respond to his work? How can I remain silent, or passive, or indifferent? I can't. So I respond with an appropriate "Amen" or "Alleluia" and more.

In worship we also respond to God in prayer. We bring him our requests, lay them at his feet, and cast ourselves, our families, our neighbors—the world—into his providential care. In many churches, however, the pastoral prayer substitutes for personal prayer. It puts all prayers and requests into the mouth of the pastor. But in those churches where prayer has been returned to the people, each individual is able to pray, to make his supplication and his thanksgiving known to God.

Also, worship calls upon me to respond to others. If in worship we realize the reconciliation we have with the Father, surely this compels us to be reconciled with each other. And I've experienced the economic implications of worship. For, if the Father feeds us in the bread and wine, are these not symbols of our responsibility to others? I cannot now eat the bread nor drink the wine without remembering my responsibility to those who suffer without adequate food, clothing, and shelter.

I'm describing a participatory worship—a worship in which we are constantly responding to the Scriptures, to prayer, to fellowship, and to the breaking of bread (Acts 2:42). I find that evangelical pastors long for a more participatory approach to worship. Pastor Neil Garrabrant expressed the feelings of many when he told me that he has begun "to think of ways of moving more toward participation, more toward expressing honor and glory to God . . . adoration . . . magnifying his character, his nature, his work, his covenant."

Fourth, *I experienced a better balance between the Word of God and the Table of the Lord.* When I was in seminary, the importance of the Lord's Table was not a subject of discussion. The majority of courses concentrated on the Word. Language study and historical backgrounds were stressed as the tools needed to unearth the treasures of Scripture. I have no regret that a strong emphasis was placed on the Word of God. I would even welcome more Scripture studies. But we Evangelicals often neglect the fact that God reveals not only through language and history, but also through signs and symbols. The living Word, the Logos, is communicated to us through the symbols of bread and wine, as well as revealed to us in a book.

Recent studies in neuropsychology have made us aware of the symbolic side of the brain. We know, apprehend, and perceive not only through language, but also through other symbolic forms of communication. For example, a ring on the appropriate finger of the left hand speaks of love, fidelity, commitment, and marriage. I believe that we evangelicals are too restrictive when it comes to forms of communication. We tend to acknowledge the verbal analytic side of our being—the left brain—but pay little attention to the subjective, aesthetic side—the right brain.

There is, however, a discernible shift in thinking which is now taking place. Evangelical theologians and pastors are recognizing a need to increase the frequency of Communion services. There are, of course, two schools of thought regarding this development. On one hand, some pastors are questioning the overwhelming dominance of the sermon. Many of these pastors agree, for example, with Bob Harvey, the pastor of Bethel Presbyterian

Church in Wheaton. "The sermon," he says, "is central, but not the goal of the service. . . . It's part of the flow of the service." On the other hand is the feeling that the Table should have a more central place than it has had in the past. Many pastors on this side would agree with Joel Sheesley, professor of art at Wheaton College. He says, "Bread and wine are a presentation of Christ in another form." What we are all discovering is that Christ is presented to us through re-presentation in *both* the Word and the Table.

But the most compelling argument for me is my own personal experience of Christ at the Communion Table. I am continually comforted and ministered to by Christ at his Table. I often counsel students and friends who are facing difficult times in their lives to "flee to the Eucharist." Bread and wine are God's signs. They are what John Calvin called "pledges," "testimonies," and "signs" of God's grace and love toward us. And those students and friends who have taken this advice have talked to me later about the healing they experienced through these symbols of God's ministry.

Yet, it seems that in our concern for preaching, somehow we have let things get out of balance. We've neglected the deep meaning of the Lord's Table. I believe, however, that as we open ourselves to the gracious working of God at the Lord's Supper, we will experience a greater balance between the Word of God and the Lord's Table. And, in turn, we will find a better balance between head and heart, mind and emotion, intellect and feeling.

Fifth, *I experienced a return of the arts to worship.* The evangelical attitude toward the arts in general and specifically toward the use of art forms in worship derives from the Calvinist and Puritan rejection of using any kind of external aid in worship. The argument which has dominated Protestant services is that worship must be direct and immediate between the human spirit and God. No person or object is permitted to serve as a channel through which or by which our worship occurs.

But I believe art in worship is a bit like the ring on the left hand. It's a vehicle through which a volume is spoken. The baptismal font or pool speaks of repentance, renewal, and entrance into the church; the cross speaks of the eternal and cosmic mystery of our salvation; the candle signifies Christ the Light of the world, and even the choir loft and its robed members convey the image of the saints gathered around the throne of God. These are not objects as such, but visual pictures that represent and bring to life our biblical heritage. Rather than rejecting them, Evangelicals are once again learning to appreciate the power of the image to communicate in the depth of our being.

Artist Alva Steffler, professor of art at Wheaton College, claims that "art in worship should be totally functional. It should not be independent or have a free life. Art is always the servant of worship, an assist." I have found that music, banners, liturgical dance, drama, color, the symbolic use of space, and other artistic objects serve my worship. They are not an end in themselves, but vehicles through which my worship to God is offered. They have the power to ignite my imagination and thus elicit the praise of God through my senses of sight, hearing, and smell.

The historic argument for the use of the arts in worship is grounded in the incarnation. The claim is that God, by becoming a person, sanctified physical and material reality as a vehicle for spiritual presence. He comes to us through flesh and blood. Why, then, shouldn't we accept appropriate art forms as visible means through which a spiritual reality becomes present or through which we offer our praise?

When viewed in this light, the use of the arts is not an end in itself. We don't make banners or Communion vessels to adore. We don't use hymns or dance or drama merely to entertain. No, all of these art forms help us in our worship. They communicate the gospel in their own way and in doing so, inspire within us offerings of praise and thanksgiving.

With my personal commitment to Evangelicalism and with my academic interests in the early church in mind, allow me to return to my experience at Wheaton College as an example of worship that brings together the evangelical spirit and the historic substance.

On the day after I had spoken in chapel, I conducted a worship service, modeling the principles I had set forth. The service unfolded in four parts: (1) We prepare to worship; (2) we hear God speak; (3) we respond to God; (4) God sends us forth. And because it was the beginning of Advent, the theme centered around the anticipation of the birth of Christ.

As more than two thousand students gathered to worship, I sensed a real spirit of anticipation and openness before God. We began the service that day by singing the glorious hymn, "Let All Mortal Flesh Keep Silence," which culminated in a vibrant "Amen." I then addressed the congregation, "The Lord be with you." Their response, "And also with you," granted me permission to pray on their behalf, calling upon God to assemble us as his worshiping community. Again, they responded with a hearty "Amen." Next, we came before God, acknowledging him as the Holy One, the Almighty, the Creator, and the Redeemer by singing "Gloria in Excelsis Deo." Finally, like Isaiah, who when he was lifted up into the heavens saw God and was overcome with a sense of his sin, we, too, standing before God, completed our preparation to worship with the brief confession of sin found in the ancient Trisagion: "Holy God, Holy and Mighty, Holy Immortal One, have mercy upon us." We were in the presence of God, formed as his worshiping community and ready to hear him speak to us.

In the second phase of our worship, we listened to God speak to us through three readings I had selected from the lectionary. First, we let Isaiah speak to us (Isa. 2:1–5); then the Wheaton College Orchesis, a dance group, enhanced our worship with a praise in movement to "simple song." Next, we listened to the words of Paul (Rom. 13:11–14), and responded with a threefold "Alleluia" as we stood and prepared to hear the Gospel (Matt. 24:37–44). "Thanks be to God" rang out after each of the Gospel readings. A short interpretation of these scriptures, calling on the congregation to prepare spiritually for Christmas, completed this phase of worship.

Now that we had heard God speak through Scripture and sermon, it was time for us to respond to him. But I was totally unprepared for what happened during this part of our worship service. We began our response to God with an anthem sung by a small, seven-member choir. Then, after leading the congregation in the Apostles' Creed, I said, "I now invite you to offer spontaneous statements of faith to the Lord." All over that congregation statements of faith burst forth: "I believe God is love"; "I've experienced the mercy of God this week"; "God is a forgiving God"; "I believe that he is." It seemed to me that this spontaneous outpouring of faith could have gone on indefinitely. Later in the service, I was moved again by the overwhelming number of people who responded to the intercessory prayers of personal thanksgiving, for the immediate community, and for the needs of the world. With the congregation still kneeling, the choir sang the Lord's Prayer in a simple and powerful Gregorian chant.

As the congregation stood from their knees, we entered into the final stage of our worship, the Dismissal. "The peace of the Lord be with you," I cried; "And also with you," they said as each member turned to his neighbor and passed a sign of peace. Indeed, I experienced a sense of real inner peace as we celebrated the peace made by the Son for us not only with the Father, but with each other. I dismissed the congregation with a benediction and blessing, saying, "Go in peace to love and serve the Lord," and we all sang "Come Thou Long Expected Jesus" with the organ stops out and a trumpet leading us in a descant. I felt lifted and exhilarated, for together we had celebrated Christ. We had crossed the barrier of passive worship and broken through to an experience of active worship. I felt confirmed once again in the sense that WORSHIP IS A VERB.

What I experienced in the Wheaton College Chapel is what this book is about. I have attempted to synthesize freedom and order in a way that will lead us in worship that is continuous with the evangelical tradition, yet mindful of the practice of those Christians who have gone before us.

In the process of doing so, I have often felt overwhelmed by the vast amount of biblical, historical, theological, and environmental material available on the subject of worship. For that reason, I have spent several years developing and testing some principles of worship that are simple and easy to grasp, but that are open-ended enough to plumb the depths and span the breadth of worship. The result is this book, *Worship Is a Verb*, which is organized around four basic principles: (1) Worship celebrates Christ; (2) in worship God speaks and acts; (3) in worship we respond to God and each other; and (4) all creation joins in worship.

CHAPTER TWO

Worship Celebrates Christ

For the first seven years of my life I lived in a mud house with a grass-thatched roof in the middle of a small village in the heart of Belgian Congo (now Zaire). It wasn't really much of a village, but it was home for my missionary parents. In addition to our mud house, there was a church, a barn where we kept pigs and sheep, and row after row of little mud huts which were home for about one thousand natives. And all of this was backed by a rather small, craggy mountain which was dotted with bushes and colorful wild flowers.

As a child, I loved to explore that mountain, looking for caves and artifacts cast aside by earlier generations of villagers. But my most vivid memories center around a Christmas Sunday morning tradition. Early in the morning the natives would make the short but tedious climb up Mt. Beli. Then, just as the sun peeked over the horizon and began to cast its long rays across the mountain, the people scrambled across the slopes picking the beautiful flowers. And, in a grand procession they would then march single file down the mountain, waving their flowers and singing Christmas carols.

The procession always ended at our little mud home.

There the people would form a circle and continue their songfest with lusty enthusiasm, swaying rhythmically to the tunes in spirited affirmation of Christ's birth. For everyone, and especially for me, it was a glorious and festive occasion, a time of celebration in which we experienced again our redemption in Christ and our ongoing new life in him.

My heart quickens even today as I recall those early scenes—scenes of celebration in worship. For it seems to me that the first principle of worship is *celebration.* It is not simply coming together in another meeting. Certainly, coming together in worship should be vastly different in motive and style from the weekly rituals of a service club, or from a corporate business meeting, monthly PTA sessions, or the hoopla of a political rally. Instead, our worship each week is meant to be a time of grand celebration—celebration of the living, dying, and rising again of Jesus for our salvation and for the salvation of the world.

WORSHIP IS A CELEBRATION

Whether we live in such distinctly different places as Africa, America, or even Russia, celebration is an important part of life. All of us regularly celebrate birthdays and anniversaries. And we usually plan well and take great care in preparing for our celebrations by creating symbols generally identified with the particular occasion. For example, we may use our finest silverware and china, and eat in a seldom-used dining room lighted only by candlelight. And as a rule, the festivities may call for flowers and gifts and picture taking—all enlivened by reminiscences from the past and the sharing of dreams for the future.

In our national life, we celebrate such holidays as Thanksgiving, New Year's Eve, Memorial Day, the Fourth of July, and Labor Day. Traditionally, these are celebrations which include family, friends, picnics, feasts, firecrackers, and cookouts. In these celebrations we rehearse our national identity and meaning, and we find the story of our lives in the larger story of our nation and culture.

These times of celebration and festivity have always had special meaning for me. They bring a stop to my world, to my frantic scurrying around, and to the orderliness of my daily routine. I am refreshed, restored, and renewed through laughter and play. Friendships are renewed, relationships restored, and ties to friends and family are deepened. And so, I look forward with eager anticipation to every celebration-event, making careful and extravagant plans and spending enormous energy to make certain they are festive and joyous occasions.

For me, worship is in many ways like these festivities because it brings the past into the present by the telling and acting out the work of Christ. It contains all the elements of festivity: coming together, story, symbol, memory, sharing, relationship, good will, giving, receiving.

Now, when I move into the sanctuary and prepare to worship, I enter into a time of rest, a time of relationship, a time to celebrate the truths that give direction to my life. My whole body, soul, and spirit become engaged in rehearsing the work of Christ which gives shape and form to my life. It is the source of my values, the energy that holds my family together, and the purpose of my work. Worship connects me with the past, gives meaning to the present, and inspires hope for the future as my soul and spirit become blended again into the drama of Christ's life, death, and resurrection.

But for so many people today, worship has become dull, intellectual, cold, formal, and alienating; or it has become, consciously or unconsciously, a form of emotional exercise which ultimately has little affect on what goes on in a person's life during the rest of the week. Why? What has happened? As I have reflected on this question from my own experience and understanding of our culture, I have become increasingly aware that the secular mindset of our culture works against worship as a celebration. Our culture makes it difficult to experience worship as a means of putting us into contact with the supernatural. Why is this so? I think it is because we live in a secular age, an age when God has been pushed to the borders of our existence.

The Impact of a Secular Outlook

Secularization must be understood as something more than violence, permissive sex, and political corruption. It is a shift in the way we see and understand things. There was a time when the idea of mystery was more a part of our thinking than it is now. God was in his heavens—high, holy, and lifted up. In worship there was a sense of awe and reverence in the presence of the One who was wholly Other. But now we have either reasoned God out of existence or so reduced him to clichés and formulas that the mystery has disappeared. Our approach to God is intellectual and scientific on one extreme and excessively "buddy-buddy" on the other; both are sorely lacking in imagination.

For example, in the pre-scientific world, truth in worship was conveyed in a performative rather than in an intellectual way. Images were important forms of communication. Metaphor, symbol, festivity, drama, and gesture were accepted ways of handing down the work of Christ.

But revolutions challenged this approach to worship. First, in the fifteenth century, came the invention of the Gutenberg Press which shifted society's attention away from imagery as the major form of communication to words. Second, in the nineteenth and twentieth centuries, scientific methodology erupted with its penchant for observation and fact. These two revolutions resulted in a moral and intellectual Christianity. Liberals turned worship into a time for ethical reflection on the love of

God, while conservatives concentrated on an intellectual defense of the gospel. In both cases church leaders gave in to secularism and allowed it to define worship. Consequently, celebration through storytelling and symbolic action was put aside for a verbal approach to worship.

Secularism has also affected worship through its distorted understanding of human personality. Since secularism lacks a supernatural view of the person, it seeks to define personhood apart from the biblical concept that we are created in the image of God. Instead, to the secularists, persons are defined in terms of economics, thought, or production. Karl Marx defined a person in terms of work: What do you do? The philosopher Descartes defined a person in terms of mind: What do you think? And the technological revolution defined a person through production: What have you done? Worship that is principally geared toward dispensing intellectual information or pressing for results—massive church memberships or decisions—has already capitulated to the secular attitude. It reduces human personality to a brain or a product, and worship deteriorates into nothing more than information for the mind or a product for the producer.

Secularization calls into question those elements that lie at the very heart of Hebrew and Christian worship. Biblical worship is rooted in an event which is to be lived, not proven. The purpose of worship is not to prove the Christ it celebrates, but to bring the worshiper so in tune with God's reconciliation through Christ that his death and resurrection become a lived experience. And telling and acting out the living, dying, and rising of Christ through celebration in worship makes the event real in the here and now. In Christian worship we are not merely asked to believe in Jesus Christ, but to live, die, and be resurrected again with him. Life is not an intellectual construct, but a journey of death and rebirth. When our life story is brought up into the story of Christ's life, death, and resurrection, it then gains meaning and purpose.

Worship Is an Antidote to Secularism

Festivity is usually associated with mirth, play, and merrymaking, but these characteristics are practically the antitheses of the Western values of thrift, industry, and ambition. Although Christian people tend to emphasize the latter set of values more than the former, psychiatrists have rightly pointed to the need for festivity as a release from the pressures of work and ambition.

Festivity puts us in touch with another realm of life—with the fanciful and the imaginative. It puts us in contact with a sense of the supernatural, the otherworldly, the mystery of life. God built into each of us the capability to dream, tell stories, act, and communicate with him and each other through festivity.

Worship taps into this side of our personality. It affirms it, releases it, and frees us to experience Christ through the festive occasion which celebrates him. In this way, celebrative worship contradicts the secular reduction of the human person into a mere economic, intellectual, or technological entity.

Certainly, Old Testament worship is highly festive and full of joy. The celebration of what God did for Israel, whether at Passover, at the Day of Atonement, or at the Feast of Weeks, is always a festive occasion.

True worship stands in opposition to the secular trend that repudiates the supernatural. Secularization says all that is, is what is. It argues that there is nothing outside of human existence to give life meaning or value. The secular attitude insists that humans are left to create their own meaning, value, and identity. But in the celebration of the Christ-event, worship affirms the supernatural, sanctions the past, and creates confidence in the future. Like Hebrew and early Christian worship, a past event is brought into the present: The Scripture proclaims Christ; the bread and wine presents Christ; hymns tell the story; and prayer communicates the posture of dependence on God.

Consequently, worship lifts the worshiper out of drudgery and brings meaning to life. Worship links the worshiper with that common set of memories which belong to the Christian family. The memory of Christ and the connection with Christian people throughout history and around the world is made through the celebration of those sacred events of the church year. This happens in every weekly celebration. It also happens on a yearly basis when the life of Christ is celebrated throughout the church year. The cycle of light (Advent, Christmas, and Epiphany) as well as the cycle of life (Lent, Easter, and Pentecost) bring the rhythm of the living, dying, and rising again of Christ into the experience of the believer's yearly life cycle. And at the same time, the secular view that life is flat, characterized by sameness, coming from nowhere, and going nowhere is challenged.

Worship challenges secularism because it establishes a relationship with God and sets the world in order. In worship, the good news is happening again. It reaffirms the reality of God, the significance of life, and the worth of the human person. It creates, sustains, and enhances a relationship with God, and it heals broken human relationships. Worship refreshes the soul, rekindles the spirit, and renews life.

Not long ago I was listening to a Harvard psychologist on the radio. He told how a number of years ago he suggested the idea that a meaningful and full life could be achieved by those who built their lives on three pillars: enjoyable work, a true experience of loving and being loved, and satisfying recreation. After commenting on these three pillars of life, he went on to say that he had recently added a fourth pillar—meaningful worship.

I certainly agree with this comment. There was a time when worship, or what was passed off as worship, worked against my inner peace. But since I have come to understand that worship is a celebration of the life, death, and resurrection of Christ, my whole attitude toward it has changed. I now love to be at worship and to experience again and again the reality of Christ. Worship is a celebration that puts me in touch with the truth that shapes my whole life, and I have found it to be a necessary element for my own spiritual formation.

WORSHIP CELEBRATES THE CHRIST-EVENT

Have you ever been at a party where an attempt was made to celebrate just for the sake of celebration? I have, and I found it to be exceptionally contrived and boring. A true celebration must be rooted in an event.

In both the Old and New Testament, worship is rooted in an actual event. The content of Old Testament worship is determined by the Exodus-event, while the content of New Testament worship is determined by the Christ-event. In either case, biblical worship celebrates the event and makes it come alive again.

The parallels between what God did in the Exodus-event and what he did in the Christ-event are striking. In both, God revealed, redeemed, and created a people for himself. A review of these three actions of God will help us understand better what it means to say that worship celebrates Christ.

First, *God reveals himself.* In the Exodus, God heard the groanings of Israel and remembered the covenant he had made with Abraham. God's message to Moses was that he would liberate the people of Israel from their bondage and bring them into the promised land. He assured them, "I will be with you" (Exod. 3:12). In this event, he revealed himself as a God faithful to his covenant. Consequently, the faithfulness of God is a dominant note in all of Israel's history and worship.

In the Christ-event, God revealed himself again. This is particularly clear in the passages surrounding the birth of Christ. The thrust of the *Magnificat* (Luke 1:46–55) is that the revelation of God has broken forth again, and in the *Benedictus* (Luke 1:68–79), Zachariah uses language similar to that of the Exodus when he says that God has "visited and redeemed" his people; God "remembers his holy covenant" and he comes "to give light" and "to guide our feet." In Christ, God's love is revealed.

Second, *God has come to redeem his people.* Israel always looked on the Exodus-event as a redemption from the oppression of their enemies. The refrain of redemption is repeatedly found in the psalms and in the worship literature of Israel, which has its beginnings in the early instruction from God: "You shall remember that you were a servant in the land of Egypt, and the Lord your God brought you out thence with a mighty hand and an outstretched arm; therefore the Lord your God commanded you to keep the sabbath day" (Deut. 5:15). The Passover is the great ritual that celebrates yearly the Exodus redemption.

And in the New Testament the Christ-event is understood as a redemption. In the *Benedictus,* Zachariah refers to Christ's coming as a *redemption* (Luke 1:68); in the *Nunc Dimittis* (Luke 2:30), Simeon says, "Mine eyes have seen thy salvation"; Jesus told his disciples that he had come to "give his life a ransom for many" (Mark 10:45). This dominant note was also expressed by Paul in the words, "God was in Christ reconciling the world to himself" (2 Cor. 5:19). Christ himself connected his death with the ancient Passover rite when, during the meal, he made the bread and the wine symbols of this death and salvation (Matt. 26:26–29). Thus, the early church referred to Christ as "our paschal Lamb" (1 Cor. 5:7).

The third parallel between the Exodus and the Christ-event is found in the *creation of a people.* After God brought the people of Israel up out of the land of Egypt, he led them to Mt. Sinai where he entered into a covenantal agreement with them. He became their God and they became his people (Exod. 24). In the same way, the book of Hebrews develops in great detail how Jesus is the New

Covenant (Heb. 7–10): "The covenant he mediates is better" (8:6); "he is the mediator of a new covenant" (9:15); "Christ has entered, not into a sanctuary made with hands, a copy of the true one, but into heaven itself, now to appear in the presence of God on our behalf" (9:24).

In both the Old and New Testaments, God's purpose in revealing himself, in redeeming, and in bringing a people into existence was to create a worshiping community to be a sign of his redeeming work. For example, when God entered into a covenant with the people of Israel, they met him at Mt. Sinai in the first public meeting between God and his people. This meeting with God became the prototype for public worship in Israel. And it was through public worship that God's revelation, redemption, and covenant were remembered and passed down in history.

In the New Testament, the author of Hebrews takes great pains to compare Christ with the Old Testament regulations of worship. Here we see that the Old Testament forms of worship find their fulfillment in the death, resurrection, and coming again of Christ. We read that Christ "appeared once for all at the end of the age to put away sin by the sacrifice of himself" (Heb. 9:26). This means that worship in the New Testament era, even as worship in the Old Testament, hearkens back to the event where God did a magnificent work for his people. It is always connected with the specific event of Christ through which God revealed himself, established redemption for the world, and called into being his new people, the church. There is nothing abstract or ethereal about that.

I was discussing with Henry Jauhiainen the idea that worship celebrates the Christ-event. He summarized the point very well: "Worship often degenerates into celebrating the believers' dedication to God. After a while you wake up and say, 'Hey, what are we celebrating here?

Not my dedication. We're celebrating the work of Christ!' "

Pastor Jauhiainen's point is extremely important. We don't go to worship to celebrate what we have done. We don't say, "Look, Lord, isn't it wonderful that I believe in you, follow you, and serve you!" No! We go to worship to praise and thank God for what *he* has done, is doing, and will do. God's work in Christ is the focus of worship. And it is the focus we need to recapture as we seek to renew our public worship experience.

The need to rediscover a truly Christ-centered approach to worship has come up frequently in my conversations with others in recent years. For example, Pastor Henry Jauhiainen says, "I feel that my Sunday morning preaching is incomplete unless I achieve some kind of celebrative statement concerning the death, resurrection, and victory of Christ. Somewhere I weave it in there as a focal point, a high point of the message."

My colleague Joel Sheesley expressed a similar concern with the Communion Table. "I would say that the bread and wine are an embodiment of Christ. I recognize Christ in the symbols and I can interact with him. I believe I'm actually participating in something real and not drumming up some abstract theory."

Both of these men have pointed to the two most important ways of presenting Christ in worship. Christ is represented in the Word of God and in the Table of the Lord.

DEVELOPING A METHOD TO CELEBRATE THE CHRIST-EVENT

Once we have come to see that worship is meant to celebrate the Christ-event, we can then move on to the next question: Is there a method for celebrating the Christ-event that will communicate the death and resurrection of Christ into my experience?

Not long ago I heard about a well-meaning minister

who was most anxious to introduce the idea of celebration in the Sunday morning worship service. At what he thought was a climactic moment, he released dozens of colorful balloons to create a festive mood of rejoicing over the resurrection of Christ. But instead, this carnival-like display embarrassed and offended most of the people. Rather than creating a sense of joy and gladness, the balloons made many feel awkward and uneasy. Instead of creating a celebration in worship, the minister's poor taste cast a pall over the entire service.

Such gimmicks are not only unnecessary, they often block or interrupt the true spirit of worship. In reacting to the use of gimmicks, Joel Sheesley commented, "I don't have to invent my worship." He doesn't have to create a method of worship; it is already present in the Christ-event. He views worship from the historical perspective—a picture portraying the drama of what God has done. "It is a symbol of what worship represents," he says. "It's a concrete form of what God wants to say to me."

Professor Sheesley is referring to worship as a drama of the Christ-event. He does not necessarily mean that we are to do dramatic portrayals within worship (although drama does have its place). Rather, he means that worship itself is a re-presentation of Christ. In this sense, worship is drama as it reenacts the Christ-event.

In another conversation, I discussed the dramatic nature of worship with Dr. James Young, drama professor at Wheaton College. Jim, like Joel, is actively involved in worship. Because his insights were exceptionally helpful to me, I want to share a conversation I had with Dr. Young:

Bob: Does worship have a script?
Jim: Yes, I think it does. But I would describe it as a comedic script, not a tragic script.

Bob: That's an interesting point. What's the difference between the two?

Jim: Well, a tragic script doesn't resolve the main tension of the play. One extreme example I can think of is Samuel Beckett's *Waiting for Godot.* Godot never comes and the play ends with the main characters still waiting. That's tragic.

Bob: And how do you describe a comedic script?

Jim: It's just the opposite. The tension or what we might call the conflict of the play is resolved.

Bob: So, in a comedic play everything turns out fine?

Jim: Yes, that's why I describe worship as comedic. The point is that the conflict between the warring factors of good and evil are resolved.

Bob: You mean that Christ's death and resurrection as the victory over sin and death are central to worship.

Jim: Yes, and central to my experience as well. I come into worship with a sense of the warring factors in my life. In worship the war is put to rest once again. God hears the cry of my heart. He forgives me. So I leave with the sense of peace and calm.

In this conversation, Dr. Young draws from his personal experience and points out the *underlying drama* of worship. He views worship as a reenactment of the Christ-event—a dramatic representation that symbolically communicates the victory of Christ over all forces of evil. Consequently, when we worship, the conflict between good and evil which we experience in our everyday lives is confronted and resolved. We leave worship once again with the personal assurance that the battle is won—Satan has been, is now being, and will be defeated. Because we are confident in Christ's victory, we experience a great release from the burden of our sin and we become filled with joy and peace.

But Dr. Young does not find this underlying drama present in many of our evangelical churches. Our conversation continued:

Jim: I think most evangelical worship services are organized and conducted on a tragic note.

Bob: That is a strange statement. Explain what you mean.

Jim: Because they don't really celebrate in the service.

Bob: What do they do?

Jim: In the vast majority of cases, the worshiper is left hanging at the point of climax.

Bob: You mean the worshiper is never brought through resolve?

Jim: Right. They don't bring you to the point where you hear and feel "Peace be with you." Instead, the worshiper leaves the service with the feeling that the world is in a tragic state, and there's little hope. You feel like your calling in life is to hang on, grit your teeth, and endure until the end.

Bob: Jim, what are you advocating? Put it to me straight.

Jim: Resolve, Bob, resolve! We have to bring our people into the triumphant sense that Christ is victor, that life—our life—has meaning in this world, now, because of Christ.

Bob: You mean this as more than something we verbalize or just think about.

Jim: Right! We have to feel that resolve. We have to sense that if God is on our side, who can be against us?

My own experience is similar to that of Dr. Young. I

have attended many evangelical worship services in which the underlying drama of Christ's work has not been central and clear. I have longed to hear the words "Christ has overcome all the powers of evil. Be at peace." But this message, the very central proclamation of the faith, is frequently missing. Often the service tells me what *I* have to do, rather than celebrating what *Christ* has done. I'm told to live right, to witness, to get myself together, to forgive my enemies, and to give more money. But that's only part of the story. I also need to hear and experience the triumphant note that God has put away evil through his work in Christ. This is the word that gives me the peace of the Lord and stimulates me to offer my life in the service of Christ.

The underlying drama described above is not the only kind of drama in worship. Let me explain.

First, *worship is characterized by a dramatic retelling.* A good Old Testament example of retelling the event in worship is found in Nehemiah 8. Recalling something of the situation will help us understand how powerful the reading of the Word was on this occasion.

The great and proud nation of Israel had been totally devastated and humiliated by Babylon. Her cities and villages had been razed to the ground and burned. Crops and livelihoods had been destroyed. And worst of all, families had been broken up and carried into captivity. (The pain and suffering experienced by Israel then was similar to that experienced in the modern-day holocaust under Hitler.) And the memory of the event had been handed down to the survivors' children who were still longing for justice and reprimands.

Finally, Cyrus had sent forth the decree that Israel's people could return to their homeland and rebuild their lives, their vocations, and their cities. But the people coming back to Jerusalem were not a religious people. They had broken the covenant and forsaken the God of Abraham, Isaac, and Jacob. They had abandoned their religious heritage. They were a secular people, and the destiny of Israel was questionable.

However, as these people were rebuilding the walls of Jerusalem, the Book of Deuteronomy was rediscovered. And Ezra the scribe, a godly man, called all the people to come together at the water gate in Jerusalem to hear the message of this lost book.

Imagine the inquisitive excitement and anticipation felt by the people of Israel. Word was out that an important book about their religious heritage had been found; the date for its reading was set; and a new pulpit was built by master carpenters for the occasion.

The momentous day finally arrived, and the people gathered at the square to hear the reading of Deuteronomy. All listened with wonder as the story of their past unfolded. They heard how God had brought them to Mt. Sinai, how he had entered into a covenant with them and made them his people. They heard the law and the exhortations not to fall away from Yahweh who loved them. And the spiritual power at this reading was such that a great conviction fell upon these people and they came to see themselves as breakers of the laws and of the covenant. We are told they were so grieved and vexed in their spirit that they wept and mourned for their sins.

The reading of the Book of Deuteronomy had the effect of bringing these people of Israel through the Exodus— through the original experience—and into a new covenantal relationship with God. It was as though they themselves had taken part in the original event.

Retelling a story is a major form of communication in both the Old and New Testaments. For example, in the first recorded sermon of the church, which is found in Acts 2:14–36, Peter tells a story that connects what is happening then with a story from the Old Testament.

Men of Israel, hear these words: Jesus of Nazareth, a man attested to you by God with mighty works and wonders and

signs which God did through him in your midst, as you your-
selves know—this Jesus, delivered up according to the defi-
nite plan and foreknowledge of God, you crucified and killed
by the hands of lawless men. But God raised him up, having
loosed the pangs of death, because it is not possible for him
to be held by it (vv. 22–24).

The followers of Jesus preached and proclaimed the
Christ-event as the new act of redemption. The disciples
of Jesus fanned out to the whole Roman empire with
the good news as Jesus had commanded. Their axiom
was: "Faith comes from what is heard, and what is heard
comes by the preaching of Christ" (Rom. 10:17). This
preaching was, as Paul described it, "not in plausable
words of wisdom, but in demonstration of the spirit and
power, that your faith might not rest in the wisdom of
men but in the power of God" (1 Cor. 2:4–5).

The similarities between preaching in the days of Nehemiah and preaching in the early church are striking. Stories were told with words—words which described and
explained an event. But they were also words attended
by a power—the power to re-create the event, to draw
people into the event, and to result in their repentance,
conversion, and commitment. According to Nehemiah,
the people wept and returned to the Lord (8:9–18); according to Acts, the people who heard the story of Christ
and the meaning of his life, death, and resurrection were
"cut to the heart," repented, and believed (2:37–38).

Next, *worship is characterized by dramatic reenactment.* God not only speaks, he also acts. Action is a form
of communication that can symbolize an event and carry
it into the worshiping community. For example, after
elaborate instructions for escaping God's judgment on
Pharaoh and the Egyptians were given to the people
of Israel, Moses instructed them to observe their actions
as a way of passing down the Exodus-event from generation to generation. "You shall observe this rite as an ordi-

nance for you and for your sons forever, and when you come to the land which the Lord will give you, as he promised, you shall keep this service. And when your children say to you, 'What do you mean by this service?' You shall say, 'It is the sacrifice of the Lord's passover, for he passed over the houses of the people of Israel in Egypt, when he slew the Egyptians but spared our houses' " (Exod. 12:24–26).

From those days right down to the present, Jews re-enact the Passover-event in celebration of their redemption from Egypt. This is called the *Haggadah,* "the prayerful recital," or the *Seder,* "the ritual order." Its purpose is not only to recite past events, but to bring them into the present. The *Haggadah* states: "In every generation, it is a man's duty to regard himself as though he himself went forth out of Egypt. . . . Wherefore we thank him who performed all these miraculous deeds for our fathers, but also for us. *He brought us forth out of bondage"* (italics mine).

In this service, words are connected with ritual, symbol, and gesture. It is a drama, a reenactment of the flight of Israel from the land of Pharaoh. It is not only a past event, but a present reality. For, although the Exodus happened in the past, its power and meaning reach down into history and change the lives of people now as did the original event. Reenactment of the action still has the power to change lives.

In the New Testament, the symbolic or ritual form of communication chosen to convey the meaning of Christ's death originates within the context of the Old Testament passover rite. Jesus took the historic symbols of bread and wine and infused new meaning into them. In the early church, the ritual connected with the Lord's Supper was very simple. But over the course of time the church, like Israel, has developed a much more elaborate symbolic action to convey the meaning of the Communion Table. Whether simple or elaborate, the same fundamental principle of proclaiming the Christ-event through ritual action is present.

The church has also retained the Old Testament principle that the event being celebrated becomes contemporaneous: Paul referred to the Table as a "participation" in Christ (1 Cor. 10:16). It is important to understand, though, that the death and resurrection of Jesus Christ is not an event which we *memorialize*. Its power, like that of the Exodus, reaches down through history and becomes a present reality to the people who celebrate it in faith.

A good example of how worship can be a dramatic retelling and reenactment was given to me by Peter Robb. "Last year," he said, "we emphasized the celebrative nature of Holy Week. We did a service on Palm Sunday in which we went from the triumphant entry to the crucifixion. The response was really positive. One comment was, 'I have not been that close to the crucifixion in a long, long time.'

"In our Friday night service we combined Maundy Thursday, Good Friday, and the stations of the cross. We started in the upper room and then people formed a procession to the front, where we served Communion. From there we went to the garden, to the arrest, to the trial, to the scourging, then the way of the cross, and finally the crucifixion.

"We used a variety of art forms to represent those events—music, Scripture readings, dramatic interpretations of the suffering of Jesus.

"We finished the service by putting him in the tomb. People were instructed to leave in silence.

"One person came up to me and said: 'I can't wait for Sunday.' I said to myself, 'That's what this was for . . . if people can't wait for Sunday, then Sunday is going to be great.' And it was. Easter was a joyful experience. Our whole congregation got caught up in the excitement of the resurrection.

"People were really excited about joining in these services, participating in an event that was happening now. The whole experience of bringing Holy Week into our present moment of life was awesome. It was an enactment that I can't forget."

I have tried in this chapter to share my deepest feelings about the importance of worship as a celebration in both our personal and church lives. Unwittingly, I believe, we have lost much of the supernatural dimension of worship, and I long for a reformation of the transcendent. Among many churches, the tendency so often is to further secularize worship by making it common through the use of popular language, contemporary music, and gimmicks. I believe this approach debases worship and makes it common and ordinary. The alternative is to be aware that our worship celebrates the extraordinary, that it should reflect the mystery of the incarnation, death, and resurrection—that it brings us Christ.

CHAPTER THREE

The Order of Worship

During my years in seminary, I had the good fortune of serving as interim pastor of a small congregation. I often reminisce over that time and savor the many pleasant memories tucked away in my memory bank. I recall how supportive, loving, and kind the people were. I see the faces of the young people that became lifelong friends; and I'm thankful for the valuable experience of putting into practice what I was learning in class. However, one memory does come back to haunt me from time to time.

One Sunday morning we had a guest preacher. Just before the service was to begin he came to me and said, "Get the preliminaries over quickly. I have a lot to say today."

At that time my attitude toward a worship service was similar to that of my guest: "Let's sing a few hymns, read some Scripture, have a prayer, and get to the sermon, the real reason for our being here." The order of the service, as such, had no meaning for me. Anything and everything leading up to the sermon was a "preliminary" and unimportant in comparison to the sermon.

In my workshops on worship I usually mention this

story of the "preliminaries." The response is always a titter, a muffled laugh, that seems to say, "I know what you are saying." Later, when we discuss this issue further, a number of pastors express a desire to create a truly meaningful worship service. I have yet to meet a pastor or worship leader who wants to treat hymns, prayers, responses, and Scripture as preliminaries. However, most pastors are confused about the order of the service and confess that their seminary training did not adequately address the real meaning of the various parts of the service.

In addition, many pastors feel their present order of service is written in cement. I frequently hear statements like, "The order of our service is a fixed ritual. It's become a sterile form, a mere path to the sermon. How can we get beyond this?" Consider, for example, the comments of Pastor Neil Garrabrant:

> We had a prepared form that our secretary at the church had for the worship service. It was the same every week. All I did was put in the hymns. So, during the course of the week I gave no thought to the service other than what hymns would tie in with my message.
>
> The service was there but it really didn't take us anywhere. There was this event followed by this event—not because they fit, not even because they moved toward some sort of climax. They were just there. Now I'm looking more toward flow within a service. My thoughts are "How can worship be the highlight of the service?"

Pastor Garrabrant touches on four matters which help identify what many other pastors are saying. First, he says, *I had a prepared form.* By his own confession the order of worship in his congregation is imbedded in tradition, fixed and unchangeable. Next, he confesses, *I gave no thought to the service.* This candid admission points out how little time is spent planning worship. Then, he admits, *it didn't take us anywhere.* Frequently our worship services don't move from point A to point B with any underlying sequence. Finally, he says *I'm looking more toward flow.* Like many of us, Pastor Garrabrant wants sequence, order, and shape in the service of worship. How can we get that?

I believe that the order of worship flows out of the principle: *Worship celebrates Christ.* Consequently, I follow this rule of thumb for sequence in worship: *Worship tells and acts out the Christ-event.* In this sense, the order of worship comes from *above*, not from *below*. Worship is patterned after God who revealed and God who became incarnate. Therefore, the twofold focus of worship is the Word (the Bible as the symbol of God speaking) and the Table (bread and wine as the symbol of God acting to save us).

WORD AND TABLE EXPLAINED AND ILLUSTRATED

Worship tells and acts out the life, death, resurrection, and coming again of Christ through the proclamation of the Word and the Table. We order our service after God's work of love and salvation. Therefore, it is an order which can be adapted to any church—Baptist, Independent, Presbyterian, Methodist, Charismatic, etc.

Essentially, as we have seen, in the ancient order of worship the story of Christ is communicated in two parts: the Word of God and the Table of the Lord. In the course of time, two other parts were added: Preparation for worship and Dismissal to serve. Thus, the most basic and rudimentary shape of worship is fourfold.

Each of these four parts of worship contains a variety of prayers, hymns, acclamations, testimonials, and responses. And a closer look will help us understand how the sequence of worship not only unfolds the story of God's redeeming love, but also brings us through the experience of that love.

1. *Preparation*
Churches that consciously begin worship with a time

of preparation, or an approach to God, generally incorporate six elements into the opening phase of worship:

1. the opening hymn (with entrance)
2. the call to worship
3. the invocation
4. the acknowledgment of God
5. the confession of sin
6. the words of forgiveness

I have become increasingly conscious of the importance of the Preparation for worship in my own life. As I prepare to worship, I kneel in silence and pray the Lord's Prayer. I savor each line and apply its meaning to my own life. Then, as the worship service begins, I reach out in spirit to everyone around me with the prayer that we may become formed into a worshiping community.

Actually, the formation of the body of Christ begins as we enter the house of the Lord and greet one another with a friendly smile and handshake. We are coming together from many different walks of life, from varying economic, social, and psychological conditions. As we enter, find our seats, and bow in prayer and meditation, the worshiping community takes shape. That body of people which God has called to be a sign of his redemption develops a common identity.

Once this community has gathered, the Preparation continues with the singing of *a hymn* during which the choir, ministers, and other leaders of worship enter and take their places before God. Their procession or movement signals that the entire congregation is now coming before God Almighty.

After the *invocation*, which represents God initiating worship and calling the body into being, the congregation *acknowledges God* in an acclamation of his worth. Then, like Isaiah who, after seeing the glory of God, declared, "Woe is me! for I am lost" (Isa. 6:5), the congregation recognizes its personal and corporate sin and *confesses that sin to God.* Following the confession of sin, the minister *proclaims God's forgiveness,* assuring God's people that their sins are forgiven and that God is graciously disposed toward them. The worshiping community is prepared for meaningful worship.

I now find that when I attend a church where I'm not led into preparation for worship, I am not ready to hear the Word of God. After all, I have come to that worship service with my burdens and needs. My life during the previous week has been rushed and hectic. I have done things which I should not have done, and I have left undone other things which I should have done. I need time to lay my burdens at the feet of Jesus. I need to be still and know that God is God. I need to hear him say, "You are forgiven. . . . You are my child. . . . I love you."

Preparation that forms the congregation into a worshiping community can occur either in a formal or an informal setting. For example, when I recently worshiped in a Plymouth Brethren Church, we began our worship with a time of silence during which I made my usual, personal preparation. Soon, an elder stood up and spoke about our coming into the presence of God. He asked us to sing "The Holiest We Enter." Afterwards, another elder reminded us of our sin, our need to confess, and our need to lay our burdens at the feet of Christ as we come to worship the triune God. Although this atmosphere was more informal than I am used to, I felt this group of people become a worshiping community as together we entered into the corporate experience of preparing ourselves to worship the living God.

David Mains tells how he impressed upon his congregation the importance of knowing that they were coming before the Lord: "I told my people that the Lord himself will be present in all his glory. I told the choir, 'When you sing "The Lord is in his holy Temple, let all the earth keep silence," I want you to know he truly is here.

You are sounding the Word through the congregation; he has again come to be with us.' When I get up to give the invocation I want it to be as though Jesus is sitting in that front row and I am talking to him and telling him how highly honored we are that he has graced our gathering with his presence."

As we rediscover the ancient sequence of worship, the Preparation for worship will become increasingly important. For through the Preparation, the body of Christ is readied to hear the Word with a sense of peace and expectancy.

2. *The Word of God*

The second part of the worship service is organized around the Word of God and consists of two parts: the reading and preaching of the Word and the response to the Word. This simple sequence has great significance. Throughout history God revealed, then the people responded. In worship, where God's revelation is made fresh and alive, it is fitting that we repeat the same sequence.

First, God speaks to us through the reading of his Word. How much Scripture should be read? In the third century, Scripture was often read for more than an hour (people did not have personal Bibles). Portions were read from the Law, the Prophets, the Epistles, Acts, and the Gospels. Between these readings, lectors would sing psalms or lead the congregation in antiphonal readings or singing of Scripture. In today's world, the commonly accepted practice is to read a lesson from the Old Testament followed by a psalm. Then an Epistle is read, followed by the Gospel. Often, a hymn or an Alleluia is sung between the Epistle and the Gospel. The sermon is preached after the Gospel. Although many pastors feel the need to include more Scripture readings in the worship service, there are still some evangelical churches that read very little Scripture.

For example, I recently attended a large evangelical

church where *no* Scripture was read. In the sermon, reference was made to a passage, but it was not read to the people. Several weeks later I was being interviewed on the subject of worship with another evangelical pastor. In the course of our conversation the matter of Scripture reading in worship was discussed. To my surprise, he admitted that there were times when he did not read Scripture in worship. The irony is that in both of these churches the people faithfully bring their Bibles to the worship service, ready to hear the Word of God.

Second, after God's Word has been read and preached, the congregation responds to God through an affirmation of faith and prayers of intercession. It is fitting, after hearing of God's love and grace, to respond to him. This is the congregation's opportunity to tell God of their faith and love, and to pray to him, telling him of their needs as well as the needs of the world. At this time, we may affirm our faith by reciting the Apostles' Creed, the Nicene Creed, or a faith statement written by the congregation for a particular worship experience. Our affirmation of faith is then followed by prayers of intercession for the needs of the world and the local community. These come after the Word rather than before, because the biblical sequence of the Gospel focuses first on God who shows himself as a loving and caring Father, then on his children who respond to him in faith and dependence.

At first glance, it may appear that this fourfold sequence of the Word can be used only in a formal setting. Again, this is not true. This order permits a great deal of flexibility. For example, a congregation may read any number of scriptures, comment on them, dramatize them, discuss, or even sing them. Likewise, a congregation may approach the faith affirmation in a number of different ways. One way is to use it as a time of general testimony. Another way is to form prayer groups during the time designated for intercessory prayer. How the actual sequence occurs is an issue for each congregation to determine.

Pentecostal Pastor Henry Jauhiainen, who follows this

same sequence, calls the response to the Word a "structured spontaneity." It is structured, he says, because it doesn't happen haphazardly; it always occurs after the reading of Scripture and preaching. It is spontaneous because the prayers and acclamations do not follow a set form. The people are free to stand up as they are led by the Holy Spirit to give testimony and lead in prayer.

Before we go on to look at the shape of worship at the Communion Table, I need to mention a biblical and early church custom that appears in many ancient services as a point of transition from the service of the Word to the service of the Table—the kiss of peace.

Originally, the kiss of peace was a natural greeting used between people. For example, in the Book of Ruth we are told that "Boaz came from Bethlehem; and he said to the reapers, 'The Lord be with you!' and they answered, 'The Lord be with you.' " In the New Testament this greeting is viewed as "the holy kiss" that Paul commands Christians to observe (see Romans 16:16). But the kiss, or greeting, takes on a more special meaning in worship because it is related to the greeting which Jesus gave his disciples when he first met them in Jerusalem after his resurrection (Luke 24:26).

In a letter which was read in worship, Peter writes, "Greet one another with the kiss of love. Peace to all of you that are in Christ" (1 Peter 5:14). By connecting the kiss with the peace of God, Peter points to the meaning that early Christians attached to this practice: Since Christ has reconciled us to God the Father, we are also reconciled to each other. Thus, in early Christian worship "the peace was passed" to each other. Although this practice was lost sometime during the early medieval era, recently it has been restored in worship renewal.

Passing the peace in worship directs our attention back to the early Christian message. It is an experience that demonstrates the community of God's people and prepares the body to move into a more intimate relationship with Christ at the Table. Some people are apprehensive of this practice at first, but once the joy of passing the peace has been experienced, it becomes a high point of worship.

3. *The Table of the Lord*

The third part of the worship service, the action and movement at the Communion Table, is characterized by simplicity. It symbolizes Jesus' experience at the Last Supper in which he "took, blessed, broke, and gave" (Matt. 26:26–29). This fourfold action is basic to the approach at the Table in all churches from the highest liturgy to the most informal celebration of Communion.

But in order to fully understand the meaning of the actions at the Communion Table, we must first understand the symbolic significance of the bread. The bread symbolizes not only God's food in the wilderness, but also the unity of the church, an image which was important to the early church. "Because there is one bread, we who are many are one body, for we all partake of the one bread" (1 Cor. 10:17). The single loaf of bread is a symbol of the *universal* church of Jesus Christ.

In the early church, the celebration of Communion was as simple as picking up a piece of bread, saying a prayer over it, breaking it, and distributing it to the believer. However, during the course of church history, traditions grew up around each action that embellished it and pointed to its significance in a more elaborate way. Nevertheless, whether simple or elaborate, the fourfold action tells a story and proclaims Christ as it did in the original event. Like the part of the service based on the Word, this part is also patterned on divine initiative and human response.

He took. Taking the bread and wine is symbolized in the act of preparing the Table. In many Protestant churches the Table is prepared before the service. However, in the ancient church the Table was prepared as part of the worship service itself. Usually, a family was chosen to walk the aisle of the church carrying the bread and wine. These elements were presented to the minister, after which they were placed upon the Table.

At this time, other families presented food and goods for distribution to the poor. Gradually, as the economy turned toward a money base, monetary offerings replaced the giving of goods. Musical accompaniment was also added. These three activities—the taking of bread and wine, the collection, and music by the choir—have come to be known collectively as the offertory.

He blessed. At the Last Supper, Jesus blessed the bread and wine in keeping with traditional Jewish prayers. In these prayers God is generally acknowledged for his involvement in life, providential care, and special blessings. And for a religious meal, the prayers are usually extended to refer also to God's mighty acts of salvation which have occurred in the past as well as those that are yet to happen. So, although we have no record of Jesus' actual prayer, we can presume it probably had something to do not only with God's mighty acts from the past, but with the act of salvation which was occurring through Jesus Christ himself.

Similarly, in churches throughout Christendom today, the prayers which are said at the Lord's Table bless God for all his good gifts and particularly for his gift of salvation. Often, there is a discernible pattern to these prayers based on the written prayers of the early church—a blessing of God, memories which evoke motives for thanksgiving, the remembrance, a prayer for the coming of the Holy Spirit, and prayers having to do with the fulfillment of God's work in history. In short, the prayers recapitulate the Gospel.

As Jesus himself took the bread and broke it as a symbol of his body, broken on the cross, so the minister breaks the bread to repeat the symbol. This gesture serves the words: "This is my body broken for you."

He gave. The final action at the Table is the giving and receiving of the bread and wine—the Communion. In 1 Corinthians 10:16, Paul refers to eating and drinking as a participation in Christ: "The cup of blessing which we bless, is it not a participation in the blood of Christ? The bread which we break, is it not a participation in the body of Christ?"

A number of theories have been suggested to explain what happens at Communion. One extreme argues that the bread and wine are little more than memorials, while another argues that if you "bite the bread you have bitten the body." Although it is impossible to give a rational explanation for what happens, it is possible to agree with Justin Martyr (150 A.D.) that the bread and wine consecrated is not "common food or common drink." Through the bread and wine, Christ becomes present in his church and to his people.

Other symbols associated with the Table, such as the vessel, the wine, and the receiving of the bread and wine, also carry important meaning.

Symbolically, the wine and the vessel are paradoxical. While wine is a symbol of joy and festivity, the cup itself is a symbol of suffering, pain, and sorrow. For example, in Mark 10, when James and John ask if they can sit on the right and left of Jesus in his kingdom, Jesus says, "You do not know what you are asking. Are you able to drink the cup that I drink, or to be baptized with the baptism with which I am baptized?" (v. 38). This is an obvious allusion to his future sufferings.

Another symbol is found in the actual way the bread and wine are received. In most Protestant churches the bread and cup are brought to the people who quietly sit, waiting for the elements. But in the early church the people stood up, walked to the Table, and stood to receive the bread and wine. This action contains a decisional choice that is powerful.

According to Pastor Loren McLean, the way Communion is now treated is troublesome to him: "I've been thinking about how to do the Communion service so that it has more meaning, yet doesn't disrupt the flow from our own tradition. On occasion I have preached the sermon from behind the Communion Table and brought it more into the central part of the worship service. Also, I'd like to use a loaf of real bread, actually break it, and let the people break it off themselves. That seems more symbolic than these neat little broken pieces. I would also like to explore ways of letting the people come forward for Communion rather than remaining in their seats. That makes them act."

I have been worshiping in a church where I've been receiving the bread and wine on a weekly basis for more than ten years. Like many others, I had grown up with the idea that bread and wine, Communion, taken too frequently would grow old and become a mere ritual. But personal experience has proven just the opposite. I have found the Table, like the Word, to be a satisfying means of nourishment and spiritual growth. Far from becoming routine, it has become like an intimate relationship. For me, Communion is a personal experience of Jesus Christ. When I move toward the Table of the Lord, I say yes to all that Jesus Christ has done for me. And, when I stretch forth my hand to receive the broken bread, I confess that I cannot live by bread alone, that I am in great need of my Lord. When the cup is lifted to my lips and I hear the words, "The blood of Christ, the cup of salvation," I say aloud, "Amen." I affirm Christ with my heart, my mind, and my whole body; and all my senses—touch, taste, smell, sight, and hearing—are evoked into worship. Sometimes in our worship, as we go forward to receive the bread and wine, we sing, "Just as I Am." On a weekly basis I'm reminded that God does accept me just as I am, that I am forgiven, loved, and accepted by my heavenly Father. This regular part of my worship has become extremely important to my spiritual experience.

4. *The Dismissal*

Now that worship has re-presented Christ and his work to the glory of the Father, the congregation is to be sent forth to do the work of the kingdom. The other side of 2 Corinthians 5:19–20 is now evoked. "God was in Christ reconciling the world to himself . . . entrusting to us the message of reconciliation. So we are ambassadors for Christ." The service therefore concludes with three very simple acts: (1) the Benediction, or blessing which sends the congregation forth in the name of the Lord and by the power of the Spirit; (2) the order to leave, which may be a simple straightforward statement like "Go in peace"; and (3) the recessional hymn, during which the ministers and the choirs walk out, signaling an end to worship and the beginning of service in the world.

THE BIBLICAL, HISTORICAL, AND THEOLOGICAL ROOTS OF ORDER IN WORSHIP

It is perfectly legitimate to ask: Does this fourfold approach to sequence in worship have any basis in Scripture? Is it an order that Evangelicals should restore? Or, is it an optional shape for worship?

Biblical and Historical Basis

We have already seen that the message of Christianity—God revealing himself, redeeming the world, and calling a people into being—is fundamental to the fourfold order of worship. By *telling* and *acting out* the story of the Gospel in our services, we reveal the natural sequence of worship.

The earliest evidence for this sequence of Christian worship, is found in the description in Acts 2:42: "And they devoted themselves to the apostles' teaching and fellowship, to the breaking of bread and the prayers." This early worship experience, which was celebrated in the context of a full meal, centered around the apostles' teaching and the breaking of bread. And these two actions of telling and doing were surrounded by prayer and Christian fellowship. Although the meal was later omitted, the basic order of Word and Table was continued (1 Cor. 11:20–22, 33–34).

The structure of Word and Table is again the focus in the earliest noncanonical description of worship written by Justin Martyr. In his *First Apology,* a letter written in 150 A.D. to the emperor in defense of the Christian faith, Martyr comments on Christian worship:

> And on the day called Sunday there is a meeting in one place of those who live in cities or the country, and the memoirs of the apostles or the writing of the prophets are read as long as time permits. When the reader has finished, the president in a discourse urges and invites [us] to the invitation of these noble beings. Then we all stand up together and offer prayers. And, as said before, when we have finished the prayer, bread is brought, and wine and water, and the president similarly sends up prayers and thanksgiving to the best of his ability, and the congregation assents, saying the Amen; the distribution and reception of the consecrated [elements] by each one, takes place and they are sent to the absent by the deacons.

The importance of this description ought not be overlooked in our concern to get back to the original practice of the church. We can draw a line from the apostolic practice recounted in Acts 2:42 (apostolic teaching and breaking of bread) to the account of worship given by Justin in the middle of the second century. We are to view Justin's record not as his own invention, but as a practice firmly established in the tradition of the New Testament church, having the force of apostolic practice behind it.

Further, this twofold approach of Word and Table is found throughout the history of the church. Of course, there have been times, such as in the medieval era, when the Table has overshadowed the Word. And there have been other times, such as today in many Protestant churches, when the Word has been overemphasized to the neglect of the Table. What we need is balance.

The Protestant Reformers Luther and Calvin advocated this balance. They wanted to see both the Word and Table celebrated at every Sunday service. This is also the case with much of early free worship. In his book *Meeting House to Camp Meeting,* Doug Adams gives this description of free worship in seventeenth- and eighteenth-century America:

At the communion table, close to the worshiping congregation, the clergy often presided with the lay leaders. Standing there with the people, clergy began the service with prayers of thanksgiving and later led prayers of intercession incorporating concerns spoken out or written by the laity. All continued to stand for singing led by the laity. Often from the table, clergy read the scriptures interspersed with exegesis so that the Word would be heard and not be a dumb reading. Then they went into the pulpit to give their sermons bearing the Bible on any of a wide range of issues related to God's kingdom on earth. Immediately after the sermon as the worship continued, they came down from the pulpit and sat at the table to answer the congregation's questions and hear witnessing by laity, who were free to agree or disagree with what the clergy had said. And from the table, clergy gave thanks and gave the bread and wine, as often as each Sunday or at least once a month, to lay leaders who distributed communion to the people. After more singing, the people often gave their offerings at the table.

Theological Basis

The structure of Word and Table is not only significant because it is supported by Scripture and history, but also because the *structure of Word and Table is characterized by theological integrity.*

Worship services that are ordered on the Word of God and the Lord's Table are faithful to the way in which God himself has sought after his creation. God first revealed. He spoke and gave witness to himself, revealing his love and concern for humanity. Then, he came. He was born, loved, died, and rose again to accomplish salvation.

According to Bob Harvey, the pastor of Bethel Presbyterian Church in Wheaton, a planned structure which tells God's story "sets the people free to worship God. It directs their thinking toward him. In a service put together haphazardly you're never sure what's going to happen next. It's very distracting." And his comments raise some very serious questions about the order of worship: Is it being faithful to Christ to throw together prayer, Scripture, and hymns to "fill in" until the sermon? Is it faithful to Christ to have an order that "doesn't go anywhere"?

The purpose of order became even clearer to me after a discussion with Jim Young which helped me put a finger on the reason a service without a story or inner movement is so unsatisfying.

Bob: Jim, can you tell me how a story usually unfolds?
Jim: Sure. Comedic drama is based on exposition, conflict, and resolve.
Bob: So there is sequence and order to a story.
Jim: Right, unless you're talking about some of the avant-garde attempts to remove sequence and plot completely.
Bob: As in a play like Beckett's *Waiting for Godot*.
Jim: Yes.

Waiting for Godot is an absurdist play because "nothing happens" . . . "no one goes any place" . . . "the play never starts and never ends." The author, Samuel Beckett, wanted to make a statement about life in writing this play. He chose to communicate what he felt was the meaninglessness and purposelessness of life by giving life no sequence or plot. The conflict of life is that the players are always waiting for and expecting Godot to come, but he never does. The play ends without the satisfaction of ending, leaving the audience with the distinct feeling that Godot will never come. Waiting for him is futile and senseless. My conversation with Jim continued:

Bob: How does worship without sequence and order make you feel?

Jim: Blah! Just like an absurdist play. My life and relationship to God seem unresolved.

Art Professor Joel Sheesley told me of an experience with poor form similar to that criticized by Jim Young. He said, "There was no point at which I could come to rest. I wanted to stand in front of a mirror, recognize myself, drop my burdens, and move on. But the order wasn't built that way."

I saw my own experience through these words and realized why my stomach sometimes felt tied up in knots after worship. Since form does communicate, we must not only rid ourselves of a poor form that doesn't bring us into resolve, but we must ask: How can order carry the worshiper through the Gospel and the experience of salvation?

It is important for us to remember that order is, as Pastor Henry Jauhiainen said, "the message." The shape of worship that is faithful to God's revelation and redemption is a medium through which truth is communicated. Consequently, the order of worship as a medium of truth will have existential relevance. Such an observation forces us to ask the question: Does the order of Word and Table communicate the reality which it represents?

I asked Pastor Bob Harvey, "Does the worshiper experience Christ through the structure?" "I would say yes," he answered. "We're telling again the story of our salvation and responding to it."

I believe Scripture, history, and theology teach that the common rhythm of the story of God's saving work in Jesus Christ is fundamental to all Christian worship. It is the framework for free church worship as much as it is the framework for the liturgical churches. There is only one story to be told and acted out. (But there are various styles, formal and informal, in which the story may be told.)

The order which I have thus described is used only on the days when Communion is celebrated. What about the order of worship on those days when Communion is not celebrated? It should be noted that the story is told more fully when both Word and Table are the order of service. However, the Word alone also tells the story, even as Communion alone proclaims Christ. So, on the Sundays or worship times when Communion is not observed, the threefold pattern of Preparation, Word, and Dismissal tells the story and meets the requirements of Christian worship.

Perhaps we should be concerned about the apparent failure of our churches to tell the story of Christ through the order of worship. Many pastors and congregations are deeply committed to the old story, yet seem adrift when it comes to the shape of worship. Unfortunately, a nonstorytelling form of worship has been frozen in place in many evangelical churches. These haphazard forms are frequently regarded as biblical, even though they don't tell the story, and relevant, even though they are dull and out of touch with human need.

Pastor Henry Jauhiainen, a committed free-style worship pastor, understands how order communicates truth. He told me, "We struggle with this. How do you insure worship in spirit and in truth? How do you bring the Gospel story into the service by design, allow for spontaneity, and achieve a dynamic service? You might call our service unstructured and spontaneous, but we have built a common theological rhythm which the congregation owns and appreciates."

The challenge this material makes to a congregation is this: Recognize that worship tells and acts out the story and bring the order of worship in line with the story. Some congregations may find that the theme of the Christ-event is already in their structure, forgotten and perhaps overlaid with recent traditions that hide rather than reveal the Gospel story. In this case, it is simply a matter of rediscovering what is present but hidden. This order is finding a growing acceptance in many worshiping communities because it tells the story and brings God's people through an experience with God.

In this chapter I have tried to suggest the basic shape of worship. There is a reason for the order of Word and Table: It is rooted in the Gospel story, in the rhythm of the dying and rising of Christ; and it re-presents Christ. Consequently, Word and Table together with the rites of Preparation and Dismissal constitute the structure of Christian worship. This is the order of the early church—an order which has found universal acceptance in two thousand years of church history.

The specific way a congregation goes through this four-fold (or threefold) sequence may depend on the size of the congregation and the place where they meet. For example, a small congregation of thirty people meeting in a home may act out the Christ-event in a way different from the way it would be acted out in a congregation of several hundred people. The intimacy of a small group in a home is more conducive to greater participation in every aspect of the service. Several people may utter calls to worship, all may pray, discussion of the sermon by the entire congregation may occur with a number of people speaking of the way in which God spoke to them through the Word, everyone may pass the kiss of peace, and during the Table the entire congregation may stand in a circle and receive the bread and wine from each other. There is a warmth, an intimacy, a sharing in a service like this that is difficult to translate into a larger congregation.

But this does not mean it is impossible. In a larger body of worshiping people, actions which are personal and intimate in a small group may have to be appropriately exaggerated or scaled down to communicate their meaning. For example, rather than an entire church proceeding into worship together in a larger group, the choir and pastors with the lay readers may form a procession to symbolize the whole community coming before God. Spontaneity may have to be reduced to the Amens, the Alleluias, the naming of prayer concerns, and the kiss of peace may be passed to only a few people where one is seated. Yet, all this can be done with as much intentionality as in a small group.

Therefore, I hesitate to tell you exactly how you should act out these parts of Christian worship. I have attempted to help you identify and understand them, now it is up to your congregation to forge a style which is appropriate for your size and needs.

CHAPTER FOUR

God Speaks and Acts

Not long ago I was threading my way through a network of freeways on the outskirts of a large city, anxiously looking for the turnoff that would take me where I wanted to go. To a stranger, the signs were a bit confusing, but after a time I took a turn which I thought was the right one. However, it wasn't long before I had a sinking feeling that I had made a mistake.

Here I was, already late for a meeting, rolling along with fast traffic in a strange city and not knowing for sure where I was going. My stomach was tense and the palms of my hands were clammy with perspiration. I was nervous, frustrated, angry, and upset.

About the time my anxiety had pushed me almost to the breaking point, I spotted a sign directing me to the correct location. And a great surge of relief flooded my entire body when, a few minutes later, I pulled up in front of my destination.

According to Scripture, the human race is spiritually lost and in need of direction. Yet out of his love for us, God provides signs to give us a sure sense of direction. But unlike the directional highway signs with which we are so familiar, God's signs are not passive. Rather, in and through them, God acts toward us and communicates his love and grace to us, so we are not left to uncertainty, despair, and frustration.

Biblical history is rich with signs pointing to God's purposes. But today, I believe, it is in worship that God gives us signs of his grace. *In worship God speaks and acts.*

This idea or principle invalidates my former preoccupation with a man-centered worship. And I'm discovering many other evangelical Christians today who are also becoming increasingly concerned with a form of worship that centers around man and his needs rather than on God and his work. My friend David Mains has expressed the concern that many people are going to church "to hear preachers, to hear music, to have fellowship." Mains objects to this idea and insists that we ought to go to church "to hear God speak." And Neil Garrabrant captured my own feelings when he said, "Our worship is too man-centered; we need to discover that it is God who is at work in worship."

One of the greatest discoveries of my Christian pilgrimage has come with the realization that the primary importance in worship is not what *I* do, but what *God* is doing. In worship, God is present, speaking to me, and acting upon me. It is in worship that God feeds, nourishes, and cares for me. And it is in worship that he gives me his grace, surrounds me with his love, lifts me up into his arms, affirms me as a member of his community, and sends me forth into the world with a fresh vision of his work and a new concern to live for him.

And throughout church history, *God's initiative in grace has always been accompanied by tangible and concrete signs.* For example, in worship I experience God's presence and action toward me through the sign of the Bible and through the signs of bread and wine, the Holy Communion. In turn, I respond to God through these signs. This means that in worship there is a descending line established by God and an ascending line represented by my faith. And the intersecting point of these lines is the visible and tangible sign of God's grace: the Bible together with the bread and the wine.

GOD SPEAKS AND ACTS THROUGH SIGNS

Biblical Sign Language

Both the Old and New Testaments are rich in illustrations of God's communicating with people through signs. The first such episode in which God's initiative of grace is communicated through a sign occurs immediately after the fall of our first parents. Adam and Eve chose to believe the word of Satan and disobeyed God. And the third chapter of Genesis contains a gruesome list of the consequences of their disobedience.

Here is a story filled with the emotion of separation, alienation, shame, rejection, reproach, fear, and anger. It was a dark moment; Adam and Eve were about to be expelled from the garden into an unknown world. They were to lose everything they had known—the beautiful garden, all the lush fruit, and their vocation to keep and till the garden. All was lost, and in their shame they stood naked before God.

Nakedness is a powerful symbol of having nothing. Adam and Eve had been stripped of everything—possessions, occupation, relationship with God. Yet, in their moment of severe depression and anxiety, we read that "the Lord God made for Adam and for his wife garments of skins and clothed them" (Gen. 3:21). Now, this may seem like a small and obscure, almost meaningless, act. But it isn't really, for it points to God's love. He loved Adam and Eve and didn't want them to leave the garden without a sign of that love or without hope. The "garments of skin" were a visible and tangible sign of God's grace and continuing love and concern for them.

Another of God's signs occurred during the days of

Noah. It seems that the whole human race with the exception of Noah had turned against God. The writer of Genesis says, "The Lord saw that the wickedness of man was great in the earth, and that every imagination of the thoughts of his heart was only evil continually. And the Lord was sorry that he had made man on the earth, and it grieved him to his heart" (Gen. 6:5–6).

Now as the story moves along, we read that God sent a flood which wiped out the human race except for Noah and his family whom he preserved through the ark (a symbol of God's grace). And when the waters had receded, God caused the ark to come to rest on dry land. Then God entered into a covenant with Noah, assuring him, "Never again shall there be a flood to destroy the earth" (Gen. 9:11). And following this promise God gave Noah more than the promise of words. God gave him a sign—a rainbow: "This is the sign of the covenant which I make between me and you and every living creature that is with you, for all future generations" (Gen. 9:12). Here was a tangible and visible sign from God which communicated a message to the entire human race—a sign of God's goodness and love.

A third illustration is found in the covenant God made with Abraham and, through him, with his descendants—Israel. Here again we see God reaching out, taking the initiative to bring humanity to himself. God promised Abraham that his descendants would become a great nation and that he would give them a land in which to live (Gen. 12:2–3). And along with the promise expressed in these verses, God gave Abraham and his descendants a sign. He said, "You shall be circumcised in the flesh of your foreskins and it shall be a sign of the covenant between me and you" (Gen. 17:11). And ever since those days circumcision has been a visible and tangible sign of God's grace to Israel. It is a constant reminder that God is *for them,* that he cares for and loves them.

Throughout the Old Testament we read again and

again about incidents in which God gave his people signs to be used in their worship of him. The early tabernacle and later the temple were filled with signs, pointing to God. The very existence of the tabernacle and the temple was a sign of God's presence with Israel. God said to Moses, "Let them make a sanctuary for me, that I may dwell in their midst" (Exod. 25:8; see also 2 Chron. 6:7; Ezek. 43:7).

The sacrifices were also instituted by God, and they acted as constant reminders of God's covenant (see Exod. 24:1–8). And the very plan of the tabernacle and temple with its outer and inner court, the Holy Place, and the Holy of Holies is a symbolic communication of a relationship established between God and Israel. The tabernacle and the temple furnishings such as the altar, the laver, the golden lampstands, the table with the bread of the Presence, the altar of incense, and the ark were signs established by God as symbols of eternal mysteries. They told a story without words—the story of redemption from Egypt, of a loving and electing God who *chose* Israel and gave them tangible and visible signs through which his love for them was constantly communicated.

Of course, we have nothing quite so elaborate as the tabernacle and the temple in the New Testament. But the writer of Hebrews makes it clear that these were "a shadow of the good things to come—instead of the true form of these realities" (Heb. 10:1). Many Protestants have incorrectly understood the writer of Hebrews to denigrate physical signs. But that is not so. The emphasis of Hebrews 7–10 is that all the signs established by God are visible reminders of his desire to establish a relationship with his people. And these signs are fulfilled in Jesus Christ who is the incarnate sign of God.

Jesus supersedes all the Old Testament signs. Now, because God has appeared in the flesh in Jesus, new signs are established to communicate his presence. The most important signs of God's grace in Jesus Christ are the

Bible and the sacrament of bread and wine. But in addition to these signs which point us to Christ and to our relationship with him, there are others, including the water of baptism, the oil of healing, and the apostolic writings. And to these we may add signs established over the centuries by the church, such as the fish, the dove, tongues of fire, the shepherd's staff, and the sign of the cross.

Significance of Religious Sign Language

For me, the significance of a sign is that it is a visible means through which the gospel of Jesus Christ is proclaimed. All signs are rooted in the incarnation of God in Jesus Christ as their ultimate point of reference. It is important to remember, though, that not one of the signs is complete in and of itself. Rather, all signs are made meaningful by the actual historical event—God made man, living, dying, and being raised on that first Easter morning. Consequently, a sign is a witness to the saving event of Jesus. So both the Bible and the Communion Table are means of proclaiming Christ.

One important fact that I try to keep in mind as I worship is that these are God's signs, not mine. The accent is on God who gives the sign of his work for us. This is an especially important principle to remember at the Table of the Lord. The fact that I take and eat the bread and drink the wine is not nearly so significant as the fact that these are God's signs through which he communicates his salvation to me. Communion is initiated by God as instructed by Jesus. These signs are a comfort to me because they bring me God's pardon and grace.

Another matter of importance for me is the physical nature of signs. A sign is not an ethereal thing, a spiritual nonentity. Rather, it is physical, tangible, concrete. For example, the sign of bread and wine is something that I can touch, handle, smell, and even eat; it emphasizes the physical side of my spiritual life. I confess that God became a man—flesh and blood, real, not an apparition. And this, God incarnate in a real person, was a matter of extreme importance in the early church and remains important for us today.

A heretical movement known as Gnosticism rejected the physical creation as intrinsically evil and insisted that Christ was not God in the flesh, but a mere apparition. Orthodox Christianity of the early church insisted on the physical reality of God in Christ. Consequently, orthodoxy believed and practiced the presence of God as communicated through physical signs, whereas the heretics denied the use of physical signs even as they denied the physical reality of God in Christ. Thus, when I affirm the significance of physical signs today, I stand with the orthodox of the early church and affirm that God became one of my kind. He became flesh and blood for me—to live, to be raised from the dead for my salvation. He shared my life. Now through faith in him I can share his.

GOD SPEAKS THROUGH THE WORD

From early childhood I was taught to believe and accept the Bible as a very special and important book. My father was a Baptist minister and a devout student of the Word. I can still picture him sitting in the living room with his Bible in hand, reading for the whole evening. He made a point of reading the Bible through once a year, in addition to his regular study of its contents.

On one occasion, when I was nine years old, I happened to see my father wrapping his Bible in newspaper. "What are you doing, Dad?" I asked. "This is an old Bible that I am planning to bury in the back yard," he answered. "Because this is God's Word, it is important to always treat it with reverence. I've worn this Bible out and bought a new one. It would be irreverent to throw it in the trash, so I'm burying it."

My father had a point. The Bible is the record of God's living action and speech to us; therefore, it ought to be treated with the greatest reverence and respect. I have found this to be true, not only in my personal life, but also in my worship. Through the Bible God still speaks to me. In Scripture God is actively present, making his will and presence known to me as I worship in community with God's people.

The Bible in Worship

I am impressed with the number of passages which accent the importance of the Word of God in worship. Very early in our biblical story we read that in the wilderness at Mt. Sinai Moses "took the Book of the Covenant and read it in the hearing of the people" (Exod. 24:7). The people of Israel did not have a Bible in the same sense that we do today. Yet, the Book of the Covenant served as their Scripture because it contained "all the words of the Lord" (Exod. 24:3). It represented the living Word of God and the agreement he had made with them.

By reading the Book of the Covenant, Israel was reminded once again that God, out of love, had chosen them and called them up out of Egypt to be a holy and unique people for himself.

I am greatly moved by the importance attached to the reading and preaching of the Scripture in this event. Apparently the reading and comments concentrated on a rehearsal of God's saving activity—bringing them up out of the Land of Egypt. Through the reading, the Exodus-event became real and alive. The event was brought to them and they sensed their involvement in God's action. Consequently, the people of Israel experienced the sense of having been brought up out of the land of Egypt again and of entering anew into their covenantal relationship with God.

Jewish worship has always had Scripture at the center

of its worship. This is seen in the development of synagogue worship which probably had its beginnings after the Exile. And, of course, by the time of Jesus we know this had become a regular practice: "And he came to Nazareth, where he had been brought up; and he went to the synagogue, as his custom was, on the sabbath day. And he stood up to read; and there was given to him the book of the prophet Isaiah. He opened the book and found the place . . ." (Luke 4:16–17). It was perfectly natural, then, for this same practice of reading to be carried over to Christian worship. Paul makes this very clear when he says, "Attend to the public reading of Scripture, to preaching, to teaching" (1 Tim. 4:13); "And when this letter has been read among you, have it read also in the church of the Laodiceans; and see that you read also the letter from Laodicea" (Col. 4:16).

The Significance of the Bible in Worship

When I listen to the reading of Scripture in worship, I try to remember that it is the record of God's covenant with us. It is a record of how God has initiated a relationship with me, sought me out, and brought me to himself.

I also pray that God will allow me to hear the Scripture reading as a witness to faith. It records not only God's activity, but also the response of faith by those for whom he acted. Nehemiah tells how the people listened, raised their hands, bowed down, and wept. When I hear the Scriptures read I want to respond in faith to the God of the covenant. I want to bow before him and worship him as my Lord and Savior.

Also, as I hear about the God who has acted in the past, the Scripture becomes the announcement of its own relevance to my needs today. For example, the God who acted in the Exodus-event to bring Israel out of Egyptian bondage, and in the Christ-event to release humankind from bondage to sin, now acts on my behalf to unite me to himself and to release me from the stranglehold of sin. Scripture is not a relic of the past, a mere historical record, but a living and dynamic activity of God's grace, communicating his actions on my behalf now, in the present.

When Scripture is read and heard in faith, its actual meaning becomes fresh and new to me, even though I may be historically removed from the event which is being proclaimed. For example, at the reading of the covenant in the time of Nehemiah, the people were told to party and rejoice as if they themselves were the original Israelites who had passed through the waters of the Red Sea. So when Scripture is read and preached in worship, it should be done with a sense of its freshness and of our participation in the very meaning of the event.

I am concerned for those churches that have lapsed into a lethargic use of Scripture. I fear that our over-familiarity with Scripture has dulled us to the freshness and excitement of God's Word. We've lost the wonder of the story line. We know the words of John 3:16 so well, but we don't really hear and relive their meaning anymore. Accordingly, we need to rediscover the power of God's Word as God's speaking and communicating to his church now, today. Here are several suggestions.

First, we must stop treating the Scripture reading as a preliminary. In worship there aren't "preliminaries." Every part of worship is an intricate aspect of the whole. Therefore, reading Scripture is not a preliminary—something to "get over with" so we can get on to the sermon.

Then, I urge that we start paying more attention to the *way* we read Scripture. After all, if Scripture is the proclamation of God, the manner in which we read it publicly is extremely important; it isn't something to stumble over and be read carelessly. Remember, it is not just the Word of God for people of the past, but it is the living Word of God for today, for Christians everywhere. It is as new and as fresh and as relevant to our needs as it was to people in past centuries. Therefore, we should read Scripture as an announcement to be heard and acted upon. It is God speaking. It contains his words of grace. It renews his covenant with us and draws us anew into the experience of our belongingness to him.

David Mains seems to agree with me when he says, "I am calling on people to take Scripture reading as a ministry of the Holy Spirit, to be a committee of one to breathe life into the public reading of Scripture. That's a powerful, powerful thing." Indeed, there needs to be a revival of attention and care for the public reading of Scripture. We need to experience Scripture as the electrifying Word of God.

Some churches have moved to meet this need by establishing a *lay readers' group.* And people who would join or be appointed to read Scripture in worship would look on this activity as their calling, their ministry to the body of Christ. Layman Peter Robb put it this way, "We find that the best way to do the Scripture reading is to get good readers. There are so many people who don't read well. We don't get people to sing who don't sing well, so why should we use readers who don't know how to read well?"

A simple announcement in the church bulletin would probably motivate a number of people who would make a commitment to a lay readers' group. It's a very simple thing to organize lay readers, yet richly rewarding to the pastor, the readers, and the congregation. Scripture texts may be assigned and read aloud several times before the service. And the pastor may meet monthly with the group to practice reading Scripture to each other. Reading Scripture in worship can be looked upon as a gift which is offered to the congregation.

GOD ACTS THROUGH BREAD AND WINE

The second major sign through which God communicates and acts upon us in worship is that of the Holy Communion—the bread and wine. One of the most difficult worship experiences for me in the past was the Lord's Supper. I can still remember the feeling of awe and fear that overtook me on the first Sunday of the month when I walked into the sanctuary and observed the white cloth draped over the Communion Table, hiding the mystery of the bread and wine to be revealed later at the appropriate moment.

On these Sundays the service was always characterized by an unusual amount of sobriety. The atmosphere was akin to a funeral parlor, and the music seemed to be more dreary than usual. The pastor's sermon was always a meditation on the death of Christ, with a great deal of time spent in quiet silence contemplating one's sin. Sometimes, though, I felt that Communion was tacked on to the end of the service, and that we rushed through it to finish by noon.

But most of all I remember my feelings when the words "Do this in remembrance of me" were spoken. That word "remembrance" always struck a responsive cord within me. I would bow my head and think hard, conjuring up the image of three crosses on Golgotha with my Savior in the middle, dying on the cross for me.

In more recent years I have come to question the extreme sobriety, the heavy emphasis on self-examination, and the notion that remembrance is something we do by way of thinking about a past event. I do not mean to deny that there is an element of truth to sobriety, self-examination, and remembrance. Rather, I wish, by way of contrast, to emphasize that the central key to the Table is not what I do, but what God does in and through the bread and wine. In short, God acts to proclaim his saving reality and presence to the believer. Consequently, the real meaning of remembrance is a celebration of Christ's resurrection and presence. The service should bring us through the death to the joy and gladness of his present resurrecting power in our lives. For, through the Supper, God acts in our midst.

Biblical Basis

The Biblical root of God's acting in the Lord's Supper is first found in the Old Testament Passover which the Lord's Supper replaces. The Passover, instituted on the eve of Israel's redemption from Egypt, was God's action, for by it God himself caused the people of Israel to be released from their captors. Consequently, it is the moment in history which all the people of Israel relive once a year as a celebration of God's action on their behalf (Exod. 12).

For centuries the Passover has been celebrated each year by Jewish families. For them it is not just a memory of a past event, but a way of participating in the event itself. And Jewish culture has created a whole family drama reenacting the original event. They dress as though ready for a journey, eat the foods prescribed for the Passover, and through story and action relive Israel's redemption from Egypt.

On the night of his arrest, Jesus and his disciples were doing what thousands of other Jewish people were doing—celebrating their release from Egypt and the redemption which God had accomplished for them. It was in the meal, though, that Jesus changed the Passover prayers to show that the Christian meaning of the Passover was to be found in his own death and subsequent resurrection.

The early Christians recognized the significance of this event as extremely important to the life of the church. But, rather than celebrate once a year as the Jews celebrated the Passover, the early Christians celebrated it as frequently as possible—probably in every meeting of worship. In our attempt to gain a better understanding of the Table of the Lord, I think it will be helpful for us to review several words used in the New Testament to describe the Table: the Breaking of Bread, the Lord's Supper, Communion, and Eucharist.

The earliest term used is the *Breaking of Bread*. It is found in Acts 2:42 where Luke tells us that in early Christian worship "they devoted themselves to the apostles' teaching and fellowship, to the breaking of bread and the prayers." And in Acts 2:46 they broke bread in their homes daily. It is generally thought by New Testament scholars that this practice had two antecedents: the Jewish custom of eating together as a religious rite, and the experience of the disciples with Jesus in his postresurrection appearances where Jesus broke bread and ate with them (see Luke 24 and John 21). In every meal Christ's presence was celebrated and the breaking of bread in worship had the particular significance of making the resurrected Lord present in the worshiping community through the signs of bread and wine.

A second term, the *Lord's Supper*, is mentioned by Paul in 1 Corinthians 11. Apparently the Corinthian Christians turned the breaking of bread into a drunken brawl. Paul chastised them for their conduct, saying, "When you meet together, it is not the Lord's Supper that you eat" (1 Cor. 11:20). He then reminded them of the Passover meal and emphasized the death of Christ and the subsequent sobriety of self-examination that was to accompany meditation on Christ's death. For this reason, the "Lord's Supper" is usually associated with the night before Christ's death—his betrayal and subsequent suffering.

The third term, *Communion*, is also found in Paul's letter to the Corinthians. It appears in the context of whether or not Christians should eat meat which has been sacrificed to idols. Here his argument against eating meat offered to idols is that it indicates a participation in worship of the pagan god. So Paul states, "What pagans sacrifice, they offer to demons and not to God. I do not want you to be partners with demons" (1 Cor. 10:20). At the same time, he refers to eating the bread and drinking the cup as a participation in Christ. (The word *Communion* can be translated as "participation.") He writes, "The cup of blessing which we bless, is it not a participation [Communion] in the blood of Christ? The bread which we break, is it not a participation in the body of Christ?" (1 Cor. 10:16). The emphasis here falls on the mystical union that is achieved with Christ through communing with him in the bread and wine. This is not something which the believer effects. Rather, it is an action of God whereby he enters into union with the believer through faith.

The fourth term is *Eucharist*. This word is translated as "thanksgiving" and appears in 1 Corinthians 14:16, "If you bless with the spirit, how can anyone in the position of an outsider say the 'Amen' to your thanksgiving [Eucharist], when he does not know what you are saying?" (see also John 6:11). The emphasis of the Eucharist has always fallen on the giving of thanks to the Father for the gift of the Son who has given his life for the salvation of the world.

From this we can see there is at least a four-sided meaning to the action of eating and drinking at the Lord's Table in worship. The four parts are:

The Breaking of Bread	The presence of Christ and resurrection of joy
The Lord's Supper	Remembering the death
Communion	Mystical union with Christ and each other
Eucharist	An offering of praise and thanksgiving

All of these emotions should be included in our thinking and worship when we gather around the Table of the

Lord. This is summarized beautifully in the simple but elegant invitation to the Table found in the *Book of Common Prayer:*

The gifts of God for the people of God
Take them in remembrance that Christ died for you
And feed on him in your hearts by faith, with thanksgiving.

Eating and drinking at the Lord's Table is an experience of God's work of salvation in Jesus Christ. It proclaims the gospel through dramatization. It enacts the death and resurrection of Christ in such a way that the senses are engaged in worship—the worshiper not only hears (as in a sermon), but also sees, tastes, smells, and experiences the symbol of Christ's death in the bread and wine. In this way, Christ is communicated to the whole person, bringing healing to body, soul, and spirit.

Personal Relevance

We need to come to the Table of the Lord with a sense of anticipation, believing that the Lord will meet us there in a unique way, that he will heal our hurts, bind up our wounds, and minister to our needs.

Pastor Ames Broen tells a story of an elderly woman in a nursing home. Recently he asked this woman, "Alma, does Communion mean more to you as you grow older?" She answered, "Oh, yes, far more. Communion has a way of penetrating to the very depths of me. It goes deep, deep down inside me. And it stays with me and reminds me of the love of God."

More and more Evangelicals are discovering, with Alma, that God is indeed present in an unusual and perhaps mysterious way through the elements of bread and wine. David Mains, for example, told me, "I've just gone through a personal study of the hymns on the Lord's Supper. Those writers understood the presence of the

Lord in Communion. When they wrote those songs, they wrote of a mystery. This presence of the Lord during Communion has always been an addendum in my experience before, but now I think it should be the focal point of the service."

Pastor Broen told me, "I'm trying to encourage the church to celebrate Communion on major church days as well as the first of the month. Personally I'd like to see it celebrated weekly."

In this chapter I have tried to set forth the second principle of Christian worship which emphasizes God's action. That God is at work in worship is demonstrated in the biblical testimony to the initiative which God takes toward persons. From Adam and Eve, to Israel, and to the whole world, it is God who seeks persons. And a witness to this search for human response is expressed through signs—garments of skin, the rainbow, the Ark of the Covenant, the Scriptures, bread and wine. Through these signs God is actively attempting to stimulate a response from people to his gift of love and forgiveness.

These signs remind us that God especially dwells with his people in worship. For this reason it will be helpful for us to have a renewed understanding of the meaning of communication through signs. Unfortunately, we have lost the meaning of sign communication by an almost fanatical pursuit of knowledge through verifiable propositions. The emphasis on verbal, logical, and verifiable truth has all but replaced truth communicated to us in less obvious ways. Communication through the language of signs cannot be reduced to logical propositional statements. It is not a verbal language. Rather, signs communicate on a more intuitive level. They express what frequently cannot be expressed in words alone. They reveal heavenly realities known more to the heart than the head. And they elicit responses of faith and trust that frequently go deeper than the human mind can describe.

For this reason, we need to recover the emphasis on signs. Although we use certain signs such as bread and wine in worship, I sense an uncomfortableness associated with them. Perhaps our fear about the use of signs is a result of the word-oriented consciousness which resulted from the communication revolution initiated by the Gutenberg Press. As previously mentioned, this invention represented a great shift from imagistic communication to written communication. It interests me that in the ancient and medieval world, where few people could read and only a paucity of books was available, communication occurred more through the arts; stained glass windows, frescos, and icons were major means of communicating truth. But we modern people revolted from imagery in favor of words as the main vehicle for communication. Consequently, symbolic language became a lost art in our culture, and an uneasiness about signs developed.

Yet, all of us recognize that we are living in the midst of another communication revolution. The printed word has been made less important as a result of television and the visual media in general. For all of us, words are increasingly viewed as one among several methods of communication. We are again learning to use our senses of sight, hearing, taste, and touch as means through which ideas are communicated.

As Christians, we will find a new sense of personal enrichment in rediscovering the signs and symbols of our faith. This certainly does not mean that worship should become a media event. Corporate worship is always something which we do as a congregation. We do not wish it to become something that we watch others do. As we restore communication through signs, we would do well to resurrect those signs which have always been used in the church.

Those congregations that have been willing to take the

risk of restoring symbolic language have found an increased aliveness to their worship. Learning to respond to God with hands and feet, eyes and ears, nose and mouth provides a break with an intellectual, head-oriented, passive, and even stuffy approach to worship. If we renew the worship of our churches, and our own spiritual lives, we will have to be willing to step out in faith and take a few risks. The rewards are worth it.

CHAPTER FIVE

Worship, an Act of Communication

It was Pentecost Sunday and I was in Moscow. For years I had dreamed of visiting this mysterious city. Now that dream had come true, and I was on my way to the old Church of the Holy Trinity to experience for the first time worshiping in a Russian Orthodox Church. My feelings were an uncomfortable mixture of anticipation and apprehension. I wondered, "Would my friend and I be the only ones there besides a handful of old women in their somber babushkas? Would we be subjected to scrutiny by the KGB? Would the liturgy be cold and tedious and meaningless?"

These and many other questions flooded my mind as our taxi wound its way along the broad and almost deserted avenues. It felt strange to be in this vast country with its atheistic ideology—its denial of God and all that I hold dear.

But as we opened the door of the church, I couldn't believe my eyes. People were jammed together, standing shoulder-to-shoulder. It looked as if there wasn't room for us, but we pushed our way in and soon found a spot just barely large enough for the two of us. Here were people of all ages—children, teenagers, young parents with babies in their arms, and older folks. And all of them were actively involved in worship. There was an intensity to their participation in the worship service. And while no one seemed to have a prayer book, every one knew the prayers and the responses.

The whole liturgy was like a dialogue between the priest, the choirs, and the congregation. For three hours we were engaged in a worship patterned after the heavenly liturgy of Revelation, chapters four and five. Even though I didn't know the language, I sensed that something was happening, the Spirit of God was there, people were being acted upon, and they were responding to what the Holy Spirit was doing in the service of worship. For me, this service was a good example of two-way communication. God was communicating to the people. The people were communicating to God and to each other. I felt enraptured by the experience, as though I had been lifted up into the heavens before the very throne of God.

It is my purpose now to view worship as an act of communication. It has been my happy discovery to experience God actually communicating in worship. He has become present through the action of worship and has lifted me up into the rhythm of his living, dying, and being raised again. And I believe that is what God intends to happen when we come together.

WORSHIP AS AN ACT OF COMMUNICATION

Several times now I have made reference to worship as an act of communication. For example, all four of the principles of worship have to do with communication theory: worship celebrates Christ; it is God who is speaking and acting; we respond to God and to each other; all creation joins in worship.

I believe that worship communicates in two ways: verbally and symbolically. And while this approach to worship is rooted in the Bible and has been experienced by the church for almost two thousand years, it is not simply a relic from the past. For example, I have been surprised to discover that recent studies in neuropsychology and communication theory affirm these two forms of communication as valid and significant means of passing information, values, and perspectives.

Two Sides of the Brain

First, let me illustrate verbal and symbolic communication based on new insights from neuropsychology. There are some fascinating studies which began to surface at the California Institute of Technology in the 1960s on the two hemispheres of the brain. We now know that the left hemisphere of the brain specializes in verbal skills, while the right side of the brain centers on nonverbal and inductive skills such as the spatial and poetic impulses of the person. The left side of the brain is more word oriented and orderly while the right side of the brain is more symbolic and creative. Now, we function from both the left and right sides of the brain, but some of us function more from one side than the other. This is why for some people the communication of words is more effective while for others the communication of symbols is more powerful.

I'm intrigued by the fact that the Bible employs both forms of communication. The Scriptures range from the straightforward discourse of historical narrative and the Epistles, to the highly imaginative and visual forms of communication in much of the Old Testament and Revelation.

For example, Paul uses the verbal form of communication in the synagogue where he reasons and debates with the Jews to come to Christ (see Acts 17:2; 18:4–9). Yet, he is radically converted because of a vision on the Damascus Road (Acts 9:3). And "no nonsense" Peter, who is much given to practical and verbal argument—"Be ready always to give an answer to every man that asketh you a reason of the hope that is in you" (1 Peter 3:15)— was greatly changed through a vision given to Cornelius (Acts 10:9–48). In one instance words are used to convey the message of Christ; in the other a vision produces such a change in the church that it opens the doors to the non-Jewish believers—a change with far-reaching religious and social consequences.

These new insights from neuropsychology have bearing on our current concern for the renewal of worship. As we think and plan toward new forms and approaches to worship, we should be concerned with achieving a balance between the verbal and symbolic means of worship so that the whole person is inspired to worship. We must also respect the fact that some people are more comfortable with verbal communication, and others with the symbolic. Since all congregations include both types, and since all people are capable of communication through both methods, improvement of both the verbal and the symbolic methods of communicating Christ in our worship experience is desirable.

It is also important for us to remember that communication in words and symbols is two-way. While God communicates to us through words and symbols, we also respond and communicate with him through words and symbols. Worship as an act of communication contains the ingredients of speech, symbol, dialogue, interaction, and relationship.

This can be illustrated by a recent experience I had with my son who was home from college. We went out together for breakfast, and as fathers do, I began asking him questions about school—his teachers, classes, and social life. I didn't feel I was getting anywhere because he responded with short, terse answers. Conversation and communication were lacking, and I felt pained and frustrated. Finally I said, "John, you make me feel terrible.

I've run out of questions. You're not conversing with me. There is no communication between us."

John, who can talk when he wants to, realized what was happening, and he obviously cared about my feelings. So he leaned back and relaxed, and it wasn't long before we were communicating, not only in words and tone of voice, but with gestures and body language. Our communication around that table became open and real.

In similar fashion I've often thought how it must pain and frustrate God when we remain passive and uninvolved in our worship when he wants to communicate with us through words and symbols, and he longs for response through words and symbols from us.

Cultural Communication

The comparison between verbal and symbolic communication and its use in worship can be understood more clearly when we look at another contrast—the contrast between transmission communication and cultural communication. The first is verbal and the second is symbolic.

In teaching, much of my communication is of the transmission type and therefore verbal. I want to transmit information to my students. So I stand before them and give them lectures on the subject. For example, I teach a course in worship. I want my students to know something about the subject of worship. So I lecture on worship in the Old Testament, worship in the New Testament, worship in the early church, and so on. I also ask them to read books and articles on this subject. So they read about the theology of worship, architecture, church music, the arts, and the church year. Now, I also feel it's important for them to exchange their understanding with other students, to enter into dialogue with other people who are studying the same subject. So I break them up into groups where they talk, argue, and interact with one another. In all of these instances there is a lot of verbal communication going on. Lectures, books, discussion, debates are all part of the learning process. In these assignments, information is being passed along, analyzed, and learned. Communication is taking place through verbal transmission.

However, over the years I have gradually become aware that what my students learn and assimilate through the transmission method of verbal communication is limited. After the course is finished, they don't seem to know what to do with all this information that is tucked away in their brains. I have come to the conclusion that they really haven't experienced what we have been talking about.

The actual experience of worship is another form of communication. It makes worship more real because it is something that is done, not something that is merely talked about. This is cultural communication. It is a communication that occurs through doing. For example, in one of my classes we were studying the human condition of sin. After class several of the students went with me to an experimental worship service which I was celebrating for Wheaton students during the chapel hour. In that worship service we had a brief time to contemplate our sin, followed by a general confession of all the people. Later, one of the students came to me and said, "It was one thing for us to talk about our sinful condition in class. It was another thing for me to actually experience it in worship." In class we were engaged in verbal communication that transmitted information. At worship we were engaged in a form of cultural communication that caused a communication to occur through an actual experience. We need both.

Recently I have changed my approach to teaching worship to include both the verbal transmission of information and the actual cultural experience of worship. We begin class with fifteen minutes of worship and end class with a full forty-five minute worship service (it's an evening class that lasts for three hours). In order to illustrate how the cultural and symbolic side of worship is communicated in a nonverbal way, let me describe what we do during those last forty-five minutes.

I am interested in teaching my students how to worship and how variety in worship can be achieved. This dual process is handled by lectures, readings, discussions, and actual worship. So in the evening worship we seek to experience what we have been studying and discussing earlier. Each week is different. The first worship service recreates the ancient Jewish service from which Christian worship derives. Then we do a second-century service, followed by a sixteenth-century Protestant service the next week, and an eighteenth-century Wesleyan service in the following week. Through these services we experience various historical styles of worship. The remaining worship services are models of modern evangelical worship. In order to experience the variety that comes from the church, each service, with the exception of the synagogue service, reflects a different season. That way we are able to experience Advent, Christmas, Epiphany, Lent, Easter, and Pentecost in the course of a semester.

I have found the combination of verbal explanation and the actual experience to be more powerful than either method standing alone. When the service itself symbolizes a church season or celebration, or when, in non-extraordinary days of the church year, worship symbolizes the living, dying, and rising again of Christ and provokes our response of praise, the total effect on the worshiper is dynamic.

I want to move now into a more concrete discussion of how the symbolic experience of communication actually happens in various parts of worship. How is the story of Christ's saving work actually told and acted out? We will look first at the story told and acted out through the Word and Lord's Table. I call these primary symbols.

And we will look second at the telling and acting of the story in the Preparation and Dismissal. I call these the secondary symbols. Each of these four parts of worship includes both a verbal and symbolic dimension of worship.

IMPROVING COMMUNICATION OF THE PRIMARY SYMBOLS

Pastor David Mains and I were talking one day about symbolic communication in worship. In the course of our conversation he said something that impressed me very much: "If Christ came physically, and actually stood in the midst of a people at worship, worship would begin with a symbol, not words. We would probably kneel, maybe even fall prostrate before him."

We would be so overwhelmed by God's presence that we would be at a loss for words. Kneeling or lying prostrate before him would say it all. It's an action worth a thousand words.

In his great wisdom and deep caring God has given us some primary symbols in worship which are worth a thousand words—the sacred Scriptures and the bread and wine, the Holy Communion. These symbols, as Pastor Ames Broen said, "reaffirm what Christians believe." I believe we need to give these symbols a more prominent place in our worship because they are special means through which God communicates his saving presence to us. Let's look at the powerful message these two symbols convey.

The Word of God

In Old Testament times the reading and explanation of the Word of God in the synagogue was a way of telling the story of how God chose Israel and freed them from slavery in Egypt. And from there the Word of God goes on to tell the entire story of Israel's history, its glory under

David and Solomon, its failure to keep covenant with God, God's faithfulness, and Israel's hope for a redeemer which was kept alive during the time of the prophets. At the very center of synagogue worship was the reading and explaining and studying of how God acted in the past. The Word shaped their worship. And it was in their worship that the people of Israel rehearsed their past in order to receive meaning and direction for life.

Continuing in the Old Testament tradition, the New Testament Church stressed the importance of retelling the Christian story. Throughout the history of the church, the reading and exposition of Scripture has always been of paramount importance, for it is in Scripture that the story of human existence as understood by the Christian is retold. We read how God created the world and everything in it. We read then about the sin of our first parents and how God acted to redeem his people through the life, death, and resurrection of his Son. And we see God's plan of redemption move forward through the church which will be his witness until Jesus returns some day to establish a new heaven and a new earth and evil is forever destroyed.

This is our heritage. Our roots are in the Word. But if Scripture is to communicate to us in our worship experience we—ministers and lay people—must personally participate more directly and intimately in the drama of the story-event. Here are four ways I believe this can be done.

1. *Each of us—pastor and people—can become personally involved in Scripture reading.* In pastor and platform-centered worship, involvement in Scripture has been, by default, taken away from the people and left to the clergy. The reading of Scripture by the clergy alone must be challenged so as to return Scripture reading to the people. One way to do this is through the use of a lay readers' group as explained in the previous chapter. Another way is through a dramatic reading

which involves the congregation as active participants. This is something more than a responsive reading. It allows the congregation to verbally play different parts of a narrative. Gospel lessons naturally lend themselves to this kind of reading. Someone can be the narrator, persons from the congregation can be particular individuals in the story, and the congregation can respond as the crowd. An excellent example of this can be found in the reading of the Passion on Palm Sunday. In addition to the narrator, persons from the congregation can take the roles of Jesus, Pilate, Peter, the soldiers, and the crowd.

2. *The Gospel portion of the Scripture can be read from the center aisle of the church.* In the ancient church it was the custom to read the Gospel from within the congregation. This action was understood as a visual symbol of God entering into human life and history in Jesus Christ. The reader may walk from the reading podium or pulpit to the center of the church where the Scripture is read. Joel Sheesley describes the impact of this method: "Reading Scripture from the center of the congregation has a symbolic meaning which makes the people of God realize that the Word of God is among them—in their midst. I find that to be stronger than just thinking about Christ's presence. For me, the reading of the Gospel from within the congregation makes the incarnation feel more real in my own life. It moves me on the symbolic level."

3. *We can follow the lectionary readings.* I have found many Evangelicals happily returning to the three-year cycle of lectionary readings after years of selecting readings randomly. According to Pastor Bill Mahlow, Scripture reading in his church prior to the adoption of the lectionary was "really a minor aspect of worship." But now he finds that there is "a tremendous amount of God's Word being read" and that the lectionary guides his worship planning for the "whole year."

Worship Minister Dan Sharp says, "By following the lectionary, the pastor preaches on passages he would otherwise skip over. I cannot understand why pastors are not haunted by the fear of leaving something out. The lectionary forces us to deal with the whole biblical story." Pastor Ames Broen summarized the value of the lectionary in these terse statements, "It gives me a sense of unity with the larger Christian community. It helps me balance some of my biases; it challenges me to stretch in ways that I might otherwise not; and it helps me in planning ahead."

4. *Congregational involvement in Scripture reading and worship can encourage the minister to vary his style of preaching.* A friend who teaches preaching recently said, "Most preachers use the same style every time they preach." If preaching is a communication event, then there is need to vary the means of communication. David Mains feels that "preaching is in tremendous need of a breakthrough." He says, "We shouldn't even think of it as preaching. Rather, we should think of it as communication. Jesus communicated in many different ways: dialogue, arguing with critics, giving people the opportunity to question him, and telling stories. People don't listen to one-way monologues anymore; we need to get them involved."

Pastor Henry Jauhiainen has been developing what he calls "celebrative preaching." He says, "There is an overdependence on a one-way delivery system. There has to be congregational participation for it to become celebrational. Even if one voice is heard from the pulpit, that somehow has to become the voice of the congregation. I cannot preach to the people; I have to preach among the people. Preaching has to arise out of the life of the people. It's what they want to say, too."

All of this is to say I believe that if the Word of God is going to tell the whole Christian story so that faith is passed along in a way that involves people, we must return Scripture reading to the people. I want to feel and experience the whole drama of redemption in such a way that the story of my own pilgrimage is gathered up into that drama and given meaning. In this way, the Word is not merely words, but life. It creates the body of Christ and reaffirms faith within me.

The Table of the Lord

The Old Testament event which corresponds to the Table as a communication event is the Passover. And it is important to understand at the outset that the Passover is not mere ritual, but it is an acting out again and again of the main event of Jewish history which has given meaning, significance, and purpose to the Jewish existence in the world. This is no informal, spontaneous, do-whatever-you-feel-like-doing approach to worship. Rather, it is based on specific forms which "live out" the event being celebrated. There is no other way the worshiper can be drawn into the meaning of these forms except through the forms themselves. But the form is not empty. It is given meaning because it is rooted in the historic event of the Exodus which it now symbolically repeats.

For the Christian, the Table of the Lord took the place of the Passover. What gives shape and meaning to life for the Christian is not the Exodus event, but the Christ-event. As God sent Moses to Israel to bring them up out of their bondage, so God has sent his Son to bring the whole world out of its bondage to sin. Thus, the death and resurrection of Christ, being the central act of this new redemption, now becomes the symbol of the meaning of our life in the world. The fact that Christians saw the death of Christ in this way is indicated by Paul's statement to the Corinthians, "For Christ, our Paschal Lamb, has been sacrificed. Let us, therefore, celebrate the festival" (1 Cor. 5:7–8).

The importance of the Table of the Lord is that it dramatizes the story of redemption. When Jesus said, "Do this in remembrance of me," he prescribed a pattern of worship which was meant, like the Passover, to symbolically repeat again and again the story of redemption. However, unlike the Passover, which was celebrated only once a year, the Table was celebrated frequently (Acts 2:42), and it became a habit in early Christian worship to celebrate Communion regularly.

What is it that the symbols of the bread and wine communicate to us when we eat and drink at the Lord's Table? First, and most important, is that bread and wine are God's symbols given to us as testimonies to his work for us. We do not seek after God; we do not do works of righteousness to please him; we do not earn our salvation. Bread and wine, which are symbols of Christ's death, are powerful presentations of one of the most basic concerns of Scripture: God seeks us out; he comes after us so to speak; he does everything necessary for our salvation. Bread and wine are chiefly God's signs, God's gifts of love. They embrace us, gather us into Jesus' act of self-sacrificing love, claim us as members of the body of Christ, heal our hurts, reconcile us to each other and signify all that the Gospel proclaims.

Second, there is a symbolic communication involved in our very taking of bread and wine, our eating and drinking. God's symbols of bread and wine are to be looked upon as objects of devotion no more than his salvation in Christ is to be looked upon as an interesting intellectual idea. No. Bread and wine are to be consumed. They are to be taken into the hand, put into the mouth, and digested in our stomach. This is the human side of the Table, the response that the signs of bread and wine call for. When we receive that bread into our mouth, bite and chew it, we are claiming God's work. We are saying, "You paid the price; you did the work; you achieved my salvation; I accept it."

In order for the Communion Table to communicate its meaning more effectively into our inner self, we need to improve its symbolic dimension. Here are five practical suggestions that will help Communion become a more powerful medium for communicating God's saving work and our appropriation of it.

1. *Put more stress on what God is doing through Communion and less emphasis on the unworthy state of the worshiper.* Since Calvin, we Protestants have stressed the self-examination of the communicant too much. It isn't that a confession of sin shouldn't accompany Communion. Rather, a confession should be made and then we should get on to the primary emphasis of the Communion which is God's grace, not our unworthy state. By overindulging ourselves in a remembrance of our sin, we sometimes get stuck at that point. Then the real message of bread and wine, which is a proclamation of forgiveness and healing, is overshadowed by a preoccupation with sin.

2. *Increase the frequency of celebrating Christ's death and resurrection at the Communion Table.* It was the norm of the early church to proclaim Christ's death and resurrection at the Table every Sunday. In the current renewal of worship this norm is being recaptured by many congregations. The old argument that too frequent use of the Communion Table makes it rote and meaningless has fallen for several reasons. One, such an argument could also be used against the reading of Scripture, weekly gatherings of the church, or even prayer, which are all essential elements of meaningful worship. More important, the testimony of those who have turned to more frequent Communion affirms that it develops, enhances, and encourages a growing relationship with the Lord.

3. *Use a single loaf and cup.* Communion is also a symbol of the church, which is Christ's body. Since there is only one body united to Christ, symbols such as a single loaf of bread and a simple cup make a more accurate statement about the relationships in Christ's body than the individual wafers or pieces of bread and the many little single cups. We are one, one with him and one

with each other. Why not communicate this symbolically as well as verbally?

4. *Ask the people to come forward to receive the bread and wine.* Since response to Christ is an important element of Communion, why not find a symbolic way to express it? In evangelical revivalism we call upon people to raise a hand, stand, walk the aisle, kneel, pray, and receive Jesus. Communion has always been a kind of response to the saving message of Jesus. Why not stand, walk the aisle, kneel, receive the bread in the hand and put it into the mouth, and lift the cup to the lips and drink? Are these not external actions which signify the internal reality of receiving Christ either for the first time or for reaffirming again and again our perpetual yes to his work for us? True, one can receive Christ without the external actions, but don't the external actions enhance, encourage, and even help to solidify that which we do internally?

5. *Sing hymns during Communion which reflect both God's work and our response.* Music itself is both a verbal and symbolic form of communication. When music is played and sung during Communion it embodies and communicates the message. The choir may sing alone or the entire congregation may softly and prayerfully sing a hymn or two together. Hymns such as "The Old Rugged Cross," "When I Survey the Wondrous Cross," or "O Sacred Head, Now Wounded" relive what God has done in Christ and is now doing. Other hymns communicate the human response to God's work. I joyfully remember that I experienced the most meaningful personal response to "Just as I Am" during a Communion service. Other hymns such as "Come, Holy Spirit, Heavenly Dove" or current popular choruses such as "Seek Ye First the Kingdom of God" express the human element of faith and choice.

In sum, both the Word and the Table are acts of communication. What we say and do as a congregation produces a union between Christ's self-giving and the giving of ourselves in the world. This is ritual communication which shapes our lives and forms our attitudes and perspectives.

IMPROVING COMMUNICATION OF THE SECONDARY SYMBOLS

Worship as a communication of the Gospel and the life of Christ will come alive even more when the primary symbols of the Word of God and the Table of the Lord are supported by the use of the secondary symbols in Preparation and Dismissal. Let's look at a few suggestions.

1. *There is a need for personal preparation before the service of worship begins.* Worship is more than form and order, well-spoken prayers, beautiful hymns, and a creative use of the arts. Worship has to do with our heart, our interior person, our longing for God, our openness to his spirit. Before worship we must learn to center our thoughts and our whole being so that we may behold God, listen to him, and internalize his message for us.

Centering is a term that refers to the intentional focus of our inner person. In worship our focus is not on self, not on our problems, not on other people or circumstances, but on God the Father, the Son, and the Holy Spirit. But too often we drag into worship all those everyday life issues that have concerned us over the past week or more. When we come to worship we bring our economic and medical worries, our difficulties with loved ones and friends, our hopes and plans for the future. We may be thinking about a business deal, a forthcoming trip, the meal that should be cooked that day, or friends we ought to call. But all these distracting issues which demand our time and energies need to be set aside when we come to worship. Our duty is to focus on Christ and what is being done in his name. Our responsibility is to turn our attention away from what we have or haven't done during the week and to resist the temptation to think about our future plans. Our calling is to be present to the action that is taking place, to focus on the moment, to center on the Christ whom we have come to celebrate. True worship demands our attention and beckons us to put ourselves into it, heart and soul.

For it is only after we have centered our attention on what is being done that we are able to "behold." In worship we behold God in all his glory. Together with that heavenly throng—the angels and archangels, the cherubim and seraphim, the host of heavenly beings— we join to sing, to bless, and to magnify his holy name. If we are to behold God, to offer him praise and thanksgiving, we must meet him and see him, experience him in all his dazzling beauty and brightness.

Unfortunately, we are often prevented from beholding him because we have not centered ourselves. But when we do center on what is being done and focus on Christ who is being represented in our worship, the beholding of our God, our Lord and Savior, our Heavenly King, is a glorious and marvelous experience. To behold him is to see him in all his splendor, to fall down before him, to worship him and acknowledge that he and he alone is God. We live in a world where the gods of contemporary civilization grab for our attention and commitment. The gods of materialism, pleasure, sensualism, and success at any cost, which plague us on a daily basis, need to be exposed for what they are. In beholding our God, these gods that would divert us and send us away from Christ are exposed and sent on the run. Worship is not complete without beholding our God, without seeing and experiencing the greatness of his power and love.

Then, once we have beheld God, we are in a position to listen to him. He wants to communicate to us, to speak to us, to wrap us up into his arms and gift us with his love and guidance. But we can't receive all he has for us unless we give him a listening heart and ear. When we behold him, he prepares us to listen to his voice, to direct our paths, to lead us into his loving will for our lives.

More than that, God wants us to internalize him, to take him into ourself, into our mind, our soul, our spirit, our will. He desires to have us so in tune with his mercy, his love, and his faithfulness that our lives, our thoughts, and our actions will be constant and consistent witnesses to his overwhelming power in our life. For this reason, it is important for us to take time before worship begins to be quiet, to meditate, and to prepare to meet our God. Kneeling in reverence or sitting quietly with our feet flat on the floor, our hands resting in the lap, and our head bowed in a posture of humble anticipation are symbols of our preparation for the act of worship.

2. *Both the Preparation for worship and the Dismissal from worship are symbols.* One symbolizes a beginning by preparing the congregation for worship through the Word and at the Table. The other symbolizes an ending by sending us forth into the world. And both the Preparation and the Dismissal should tell a story.

The Preparation is frequently called the Approach because it tells the story of how we come before God. Therefore, the manner in which we come before God will speak as clearly as the words of our coming.

For example, Jim Young describes the Preparation for worship in this way:

For me, worship is the drama of human experience. Through worship my world is put back into order, my life regains its meaning, my focus is restored. When I come into worship I don't want to begin with something joyful and bubbly. I'm there as a fragmented person. I bring my troubles, my conflicts, my lostness, my inadequacy. What I want to do is establish my need, confess my sin, hear God's peace. This brings me through a crisis point so I can sit back and hear God speak to me and commune with him. Then I leave full of joy.

Jim Young's point is very important. If life and worship are to come together, it is important that in planning our worship we give careful attention to our movement from the point of our deep need to being ready and prepared to hear God's Word. Every act of preparation should help move us into the adventure of worship—into the story of God at work. And that includes our attitudes, our words, and the nonverbal expressions of our bodies.

In a similar way, the Dismissal tells a story. It is more than a signal that the time of worship is over. It is the beginning of service in the world. The content of the Dismissal, although brief, should be well thought through. With this in mind, many pastors are now giving more thought to the benediction. One pastor has memorized Scripture that is appropriate to the church in the world. He always weaves this into his benediction in a proclamatory sense and ties it into the life of his people. I've heard him proclaim, "You are the salt of the earth . . . go and be salt in your home . . . love your spouse and children; be salt at work . . . be honest in your business dealings." In this proclamation, benediction and dismissal are combined, carefully and thoughtfully, to tie worship into life.

Most churches also have some kind of recessional which signals going forth. Pastor Ames Broen, for example, tells how the church where he recently became pastor had observed an interesting dismissal sign. As the pastor before him walked the central aisle to the back of the church, he always stopped for his wife who then walked out with him. When Broen first became pastor of the church, he and his wife chose not to follow this practice. One Sunday an elderly man came to him and said, "I wish you would bring your wife down the aisle. It doesn't feel like the service ends anymore." Pastor Broen said, "I then realized how important this traditional symbol was to those people. Now we walk the aisle together and the people smile approvingly." The people liked this because for them it told a story, not only of going forth, but in going forth as a family—a symbol very important to a congregation that considers itself to be family-oriented. This may not be the appropriate symbol for every congregation, but it illustrates the importance of the Dismissal and the need to give careful thought to the words and actions that send God's people into the world.

3. *Body language is a significant secondary symbol in worship.* In all four parts of worship the body language of the people of God should symbolize our attitudes and correspond to the words being spoken. In most Protestant churches, the body is invited only to walk to the pew, sit, and stand for the hymns. The exception to this limited involvement is found in some charismatic churches where worshipers engage in a freer participation through the raising of hands and a more open response to the rhythm of the music.

There are, of course, many ways our body language in worship can bring some form of action to our words. Let's look at just a few of them. First, during the Preparation for worship the congregation can bow in prayer and meditation. This is a posture of humility and a gesture of readiness. It signals a contrite spirit and an open heart that is ready and willing to come before God to receive his forgiveness and to offer him praise and thanksgiving.

Second, everyone can stand and listen prayerfully during the reading of the Gospel. Naturally, we all listen attentively and respectfully when any portion of the Word of God is being read, but special respect is paid to the Gospel reading because it, more than other Scriptures, is a symbol of the incarnation.

Third, we can kneel during the prayers of intercession. Dan Sharp tells of his experience at Grace Chapel in Lexington, Massachusetts. "One of the first Sundays that I asked everyone to kneel during the prayer, some people came to me with tears in their eyes, thanking me. One said, 'Now that I know Christ, kneeling takes on a whole new context.'" Dr. Sharp went on to say, "In the next sanctuary we build, kneelers are a very obvious thing to put in."

Another use of the body employed by many churches is "passing the peace." This is a joyful event because it signals the presence of God's peace in the heart and among the people. So, as we turn and greet each other with the words "the peace of the Lord be with you," accompanied by a cordial handshake, we send a warm message of caring to those around us.

And finally, the body becomes an expression of worship as we walk to the Communion Table and then kneel to receive the bread and the wine. This is a powerful act, symbolic of our desire to receive Christ.

Any and all bodily gestures in worship should be done with intention and purpose. They are not mere external trappings, but are ways of bringing external actions in line with internal feelings.

In this chapter we have viewed worship as an act of communication. And worship as an act of communication evangelizes me. What is being proclaimed to the glory of the Father is Jesus Christ and his work of salvation (see Rev. 4 and 5). Consequently, as a worshiper I am being carried through the experience of hearing and seeing Christ proclaimed and acted out. And more, I am called upon to act in constant response to the Good News. Therefore, worship is a continuation of the salvation event; it has the effect of changing our lives, of forming us into the new creation, of giving shape to our Christian world view and of determining our patterns of ethical behavior.

Further, worship as a communication event educates me in the Christian life. The full gamut of Scriptures read and preached forms my entire life in the world— personal, family, vocation, ethical. In this way worship sets the world in order, educates me about my place in it, and inspires me to understand God's ways of dealing with me and with his people.

Finally, worship forms me spiritually. Worship not only presents Christ, it causes Christ to be formed in my life. The structure of worship is itself the structure of life—words and deeds. When I am thoroughly involved in worship I not only hear and see, but I become. I am to become God's Word and God's Bread to the world. To be formed by worship is to take on the characteristics of Christ, to be shaped by his presence within.

As we have seen, in the process of worshiping, our spiritual education and growth occurs through both word and symbol. By symbolizing what we say, the reality of coming into personal contact with God in worship is experienced not only in the mind, but also in the heart, in the will, in the emotions, and by the senses. Our whole person is drawn into the very presence of God, and all our being—our bodies, our sight, our hearing, our tasting, and our sense of smell—become alive with worship and praise. We become an "Alleluia" to the Lord, a living experience of "Thanks be to God."

CHAPTER SIX

We Respond to God and Each Other

When I was a boy my father took me to a war rally to hear an address by a five-star general. Instead of hurrying out of the hall when the meeting was over, we stood in an aisle watching the flurry of excitement that surrounded the general and his party. It wasn't long before he began to move right up the aisle in our direction. My heart began to pound as I realized that this important man was going to pass very close to where we were standing. And as he came up to where we were, he stopped suddenly and looked at me. Then, with a friendly smile he patted me on the head and shook my hand and asked my name. I was so awe-struck by his uniform and ribbons that I ducked my head and just stuttered. My mouth was so dry that my words just wouldn't come out.

When we got home, my father scolded me for not responding properly to the general. And then he went on to explain how to meet a dignitary. Even now I can remember his words. "Son," he said, "when anyone talks to you, stand up straight, look him in the eye, and speak right up. You must learn to respond properly when you meet people."

As I have reflected on this incident and the lesson I

learned that night, I see just how important our response is when we meet God in worship. Response is a necessary element in the communication that takes place at worship. It is the complement to God's speaking and acting. It is, as Pastor Henry Jauhiainen said, "putting an Amen to God . . . owning what he says and does."

OUR RESPONSE DESCRIBED

I have come to believe that, essentially, worship cannot take place without *our* response to God himself, wherein our innermost selves reach out to him. For example, in worship we aren't responding to circumstances and situations in the church or in the world, or to values such as goodness and mercy. As a matter of fact, we are not even responding to life itself. Rather, our response is to God— God the Father, God the Son, and God the Holy Spirit. And for me, this response is an awesome and holy aspect of worship. As my friend Pastor David Mains put it, "Even though we're not very good at it, we are asking God to listen as we attempt to pour out our feelings of adoration and praise."

We Respond to God Himself

I find myself deeply moved in reverence and humility whenever I realize that in worship I am responding to the almighty and ever-living God who is transcendent, the God who pervades the limitless universe. It is intensely sobering to realize that we worship the God who is "wholly other," the Almighty Creator, the Holy One, the King and Ruler of all.

We worship the same God who, when he entered into covenant with Israel, allowed only Moses to set foot on and to climb to the top of Sinai. The rest of the people were not even allowed to touch the mountain. Rather, they huddled together in fear and trembled as thunder and lightning signaled the presence of the eternal God. It seems to me, though, that we twentieth-century Christians have perhaps unconsciously lost something that is extremely important in our worship experience— a recognition that the One before whom we stand is Almighty God. St. John Chrysostom, a fourth-century bishop from Constantinople, wrote in colorful prose about the insolence and audacity of those who pretended to comprehend the mystery of Almighty God. "We *insult* God," he says, "when we do not recognize him in his transcendent majesty. What of the angels, the cherubim, and seraphim? Do they reason about the nature of God? No, they fall down and worship him with great trembling." If these creatures of heaven live before God in an unceasing posture of praise and adoration, how can we mortal beings act lightly and imprudently before him in worship?

For me, the recognition of God's majesty speaks against any over-familiarity with God. Like so many Evangelicals today, I tend to ignore the distance between me and God and have replaced it with an over-emphasis on God as my friend, my buddy. For too many years I acted with a comfortable nonchalance both before and during the service of worship. But I now believe that an awareness of God's transcendence demands that we recover a sense of the majesty of God in our worship services. This will call for a revolution of consciousness whereby we change our perception of God and our habits of relating to him. And in doing so, we will recover the true spirit of worship which dominated the Church in the New Testament days and continued on for years—even centuries—of Christian history. This is nothing new, but rather a recovery of our heritage.

We Respond to God's Actions

In worship we not only respond to God himself, but also to his actions for us and the church. And even though we may not know God in his essence, which is beyond our human comprehension, we can know him through his actions. We can worship him for his works in the world which we understand somewhat and relate to however feebly.

In the Old Testament, God was and is known to Israel through the action of the Exodus; and in the New Testament, God is known to the church through the action of the Christ-event. Each of these is an action of God which demands a response. In both the Old Testament and the New Testament that response is the birth of a people. The Exodus produced the nation of Israel, and the cross gave birth to the church.

The birth of the church is a worship-event because it is the primary response to the work of Christ. The church is also the context in which the Christ-event continues to be proclaimed, even now, in the Word and acted out at the Communion Table. And Christ's promise of the Holy Spirit, the experience of the early church, and select images of the church support the worshiping community as the focus of response.

First, in the New Testament, Christ's promise and *the coming of the Holy Spirit* provide us with a good illustration of response. In his Gospel, John wrote that Jesus, in the days prior to his death, said, "The Counselor, the Holy Spirit, whom the Father will send in my name, he will teach you all things, and bring to your remembrance all that I have said to you" (John 14:26). And in the second chapter of Acts we read how the Spirit came to that small band of disciples, who, although they did not know it, already constituted the church. The presence of God the Holy Spirit came upon this little church and gave them understanding and power. They, in turn, responded to the Holy Spirit by proclaiming Jesus as Messiah (Acts 2:36), and so powerful was their response that, after Peter's electrifying sermon, about three thousand people were converted and became a part of the church of God (Acts 2:41).

I am convinced that God intends for our worship today to be accompanied by a powerful presence and working of the Holy Spirit. I am not suggesting that the initial coming of the Holy Spirit at Pentecost was not unique. It was. In fact, it resulted in the beginning of the church as a historical and visible group of people. What I believe, and believe with all my heart, is the possibility of a fresh visitation of the Holy Spirit's presence and power each time we worship.

Don't get me wrong. I'm not saying there will be rushing winds or tongues of fire. And I don't expect three thousand people to walk the aisle. But I do believe worship in our contemporary evangelical churches can move beyond the dry, intellectual, mechanical forms and evoke within us a sense of awe, adoration, thankfulness, and downright enthusiasm for what God has done for us.

Second, look at *the experience of the early Christian community.* Luke tells us that "they devoted themselves to the apostles' teaching and fellowship, to the breaking of bread, and the prayers" (Acts 2:42). "Everyone," he says, "was filled with awe." In their worship the presence of the triune God was felt in a tangible and material way. God was present in the apostles (whom Christ had appointed), in fellowship (the new community of God's people), in the breaking of the bread (the earliest remembrance of the Last Supper), and in prayer (personal communion). It is no wonder that the early Christians were struck with "awe." They experienced the new way in which God made himself present in their own bodies—the temples of God—and in the believers (whom Paul later identified as the body of Christ).

This is an incredible description of response—people experiencing awe and wonder. But this passage also reminds me of my own propensity toward a more measurable response. Like many Evangelicals, I want to see numbers. I'm impressed by crowds, by a "no seats left" sanctuary. What Luke is describing, however, is not a response with a lot of hoopla or pep rally enthusiasm.

Rather, it is a response that goes deep into the very inner chambers of the person—a response that touches our hearts and emotions and makes us feel awe-struck. We feel the mystery and experience of the power touching us in a warm and healing manner.

I believe this kind of response which is motivated by the Holy Spirit can happen in our churches today. But we have to create an atmosphere in which it can happen. We need to let go of our intellectual idea of worship and realize there is more to worship than a sermon; we have to let go of our evangelistic notion of worship and reckon with the fact that worship is not primarily directed toward the sinners who need to be converted; we must let go of our entertainment expectations and remind ourselves that we are not in church to watch a Christian variety show.

We have gathered together in worship to be met by God the Almighty. God, the Creator of the universe, the One who sustains our lives, our Redeemer and King, is present through proclamation and remembrance. He wants to communicate to us, to penetrate our inner self, to take up residence within us. And, as we go through the experience of meeting with him in this mystical moment of public worship, we are to respond.

But response is not just singing a hymn, not just saying a creed, not just saying a prayer. Response, from the very beginning of worship to the end, must be a powerful inner experience of actually being in the presence of God. When we sing a hymn or say a confession or prayer, we are not singing or saying words, but expressing a feeling, baring our souls, truly responding and communicating to the living and active presence of a loving and merciful God.

Third, I find the *New Testament images of our relationship with God in worship* teach and advocate a mystical, inner experience of awe and wonder in worship.

For example, the image of the church as the "bride

of Christ" is an image that strikes at the heart of our mystical response to God in worship. Everyone loves a wedding. Personally, the drama of a wedding always moves me in my inner self to the point of tears. Somehow the power of a marriage-event gets inside of me and arouses feelings of awe and reverence. The sheer mystery of two people becoming united as one, a mystery which I cannot completely grasp intellectually, is always a powerful experience for me.

Worship can be like that too. The image of the "bride" in both the Old and New Testaments emphasizes the mystery of God's nearness. He who is high, holy, and lifted up is so near to his people, the church, that their relationship can be described as that of a bride and a groom. (See John 3:29; Matt. 9:15, 22:2ff., 25:1–10; 2 Cor. 11:12; Eph. 5:25–32).

Recently I was a guest at a large wedding in an evangelical church. When I entered the sanctuary to take my seat I was immediately struck by the symbols of what was to take place. I was greeted by a young man decked out in a handsome tuxedo. The light gray jacket fit his trim body like a glove. And the dark gray, pin-striped trousers, which touched perfectly the tip of his shiny black shoes, were neatly pressed. He smiled at me and took me to my seat, making me feel welcome. I sat in the middle of the church on the bride's side. While I was sitting there, I looked around me and took notice of all the symbols of this important event. The sanctuary was full of flowers, ferns, and candles. In the front, large green ferns stood to either side of the red cushioned kneeler where the bride and groom would soon kneel to pray after their vows. Behind the kneeler were candelabras with numerous candles waiting to be lit. I looked down the aisle to see a special flower, fern, and candle arrangement neatly mounted on the end of each pew all the way down the aisle on both sides. The atmosphere was charged with anticipation and expectation, and I could feel it lifting me up into the event that was about to occur.

As we approached the appointed hour, more signs of the event appeared in rapid succession as preparation for the meeting of the bride and groom: someone sang hymns of love and joy; the mothers were escorted to their places with great pomp and ceremony; two of the ushers walked to the prayer bench, gathered up the ends of the long white runway for the wedding party, and rolled it down the aisle, signaling the end of the seating and the beginning of the bridal procession.

As the organ music signaled the entrance of the wedding party, all eyes turned to watch the groom and his entourage take their places. Then all our attention became fixed on the bride's party. We all watched with beaming pride as each lovely attendant slowly walked the aisle, took her place, and turned toward the back with full expectancy of the coming of the bride.

Finally the moment came. The organ began the wedding march, the congregation stood, and there in all her dazzling and radiant beauty was the bride on her father's arm, being carried, as it were, to meet the groom. As usual, my heart was in my throat, my mouth was dry, my eyes were moist, and I felt like I would burst with excitement and anticipation.

At that very moment I felt a tremendous sadness well up within me. But the sadness had nothing to do with the wedding. It had to do with worship. I was reminded of my worship experiences in that very church, a church where worship is intellectual, dry, and lacking in imagination. I thought to myself, "This church will do all this to emphasize the importance of the marriage between a man and a woman. Yet, when it comes to worship, nothing special is permitted." In that church, as in many evangelical churches, the use of the external to help prompt a response of the heart to God is not permitted. Candles, decorations, processions, symbols of celebration, special clothing are all seen as external pomp and ceremony having nothing to do with the inner person's response.

I wonder what would happen in our worship services if we would exercise our imagination a bit—stretch it perhaps to fulfill this biblical image that worship is like the bride coming to the wedding feast to meet the groom. I suspect the nature of our response in worship would change from passive inattention to active and attentive participation.

I'm not saying that we *have* to have candles and all the ceremonial that made that wedding special. These symbols will not restore worship. What I am saying is that we must once again pay attention to the image of what we are about in worship. We need to recover an inner experience of worship and a feeling for the majesty of God when we gather to proclaim Christ and to dramatize his death and resurrection to the glory of the Father. If we do that, I feel certain that we will find ways to increase awe, reverence, and a sense of mystery and wonder at the action taking place in worship.

If the reenactment of our relationship to God is of any importance to us at all, we will find ways within our tradition to break free from the casual, and sometimes irreverent approach we take to worship.

SPONTANEOUS RESPONSE

We Respond to the Specific

The wedding illustration helps me understand better the principle that response is always related to something specific and concrete. We are all creatures of response. We respond to our spouse, our children, our employer or employees, our neighbors. We may also respond to a sunset, to a gift, to another person's anger, to an expression of love, or to two people uniting their lives in matrimony. Our response may be that of anger, joy, frustration, sadness, or cheerfulness.

And what is true in life in general is true in worship. Worship is a response to someone and to something that happened. We respond to God—to who he is and to what he has done for us in Jesus Christ—through the external signs that represent him. At the wedding I responded to tangible symbols like flowers, candles, music, tuxedos, gowns, the procession, the exchange of vows, the kiss, the recessional, the receiving line, and the reception. Similarly, in worship I respond to God through external rites such as song, prayer, Scripture, and Communion Table. For me, such symbols have the power to recollect a past event.

Even as the Passover has the power to recreate the Exodus-event for the people of Israel, so our worship today must be characterized by evocative symbols which recollect the Christ-event. Worship is not for the purpose of remembering the reformation, hailing the founding of America, saluting mothers, boy scouts, girl scouts, or grandparents. Worship does not celebrate Independence Day, Memorial Day, or Labor Day. No. Worship remembers the birth, life, death, and resurrection of Jesus Christ. Therefore, the symbols, the rites, the order, and all that goes into an actual service of worship must pertain to the event of God revealing himself to us, becoming incarnate in our history, and redeeming us from the power of the evil one, setting us free to enjoy him forever.

My point is this. Response in worship, as it is in any other situation, is a response to something specific. I respond in worship to God whose person and work of redemption is represented to me through what is being done. Let me give you an example.

Recently I conducted a weekend retreat on worship for the Harvard Graduate Student Christian Fellowship Group at the Glastonbury Abbey in Hingham, Massachusetts. This was a perfect setting for the retreat because the monks worship before breakfast, at noon, in the late afternoon, and in the evening. We were invited to worship with them. And we did.

Glastonbury is a renewal abbey. The monks have a vital personal relationship with Jesus Christ. They all have an unusual amount of joy and peace which I felt even in my conversation with them. This serenity of theirs, and its accompanying love and warmth, draws people from miles around to attend their worship.

When I first met them, I wondered, "What is the key to their joy?" It didn't take me long to find out. The clue was in their worship which did not emphasize "my faith," "my commitment," or "what I am doing for God." Rather, it emphasized "what God has done for me."

One specialty at the Glastonbury Abbey was the singing of psalms which we did several times a day. These psalms concentrated on God's love, his faithfulness, his tender care and mercy. While the psalms still ring in my heart, what comes back to my mind almost every day is a refrain that was sung in the Sunday liturgy: "The Lord is full of loving kindness." Of course I've heard that refrain many times before, but somehow during that service and in that setting that truth grasped me. I wasn't asked to understand it or even to respond to it. It was simply there as a proclamation from God. It came after me like the hound of heaven. It wrapped its arms around me and held me tight. It entered into my heart and soul and penetrated into every part of my being. I was in its grip. And I felt overwhelmed by God's love and care for me. I responded to my awe with "Alleluia," "Amen," "Thanks be to God," although no one had told me to. The power of the message was so overwhelming that my response was a spontaneous joy, followed by a flood of peace that swept over my soul.

My experience at the Glastonbury Abbey illustrates two characteristics of response in worship. The first is that response is always to something specific and concrete.

The second is that response is not a mere ritual, a mechanical affirmation of what has been said or done. Rather, it arises from the heart, from the innermost part of our being. It is more than a mere intellectual acquiescence. It is a feeling, an emotion that arises from the interior of our person.

My experience at the Glastonbury Abbey also helps me understand the relationship between freedom and order in worship. It is very similar to what I experienced at the wedding. I responded specifically to the wedding-event because I was there not only as a witness to the event, but as a participant through an emotional unity with what was happening.

Although worship dramatizes an event which happened long ago, it brings that event into the present by the power of the Holy Spirit. In each worship experience, I am present in the actual event. Each worship experience contains the fullness of the birth, life, teachings, ministry, death, resurrection, and promised return of Christ. The rites evoke the historical event and bring it into the present. So, for example, on Christmas I am present at the birth of Christ; on Epiphany I am there at the presentation of Christ; on Maundy Thursday I am present at the Last Supper; on Good Friday I am taken to the cross and put into the tomb; on Easter I stand at the empty tomb; and on Pentecost Sunday I receive the Holy Spirit.

The re-presentation of these events are ordered. The content is fixed by the event which it re-creates. This content cannot be changed or altered. It is there as a historical occurrence, something that happened in history that is now being re-presented through reenactment. Spontaneity occurs through my response, through what I feel, and through what I say and do as a result of that inward response to God that is now evoked by the remembrance made real in the ordered events of the worship service.

Spontaneity in worship is, therefore, not worship without order, but response to God and to his works in history for us in an ordered and sequential way. We are part of the dramatic rehearsal of the Christ-event. And our response is an integral part of the actual re-creation of the event.

Examples of Response

I have attempted to show how the fourfold shape of worship (Preparation, Word, Table, Dismissal) re-presents God and his saving work in Christ. This is an order to the service of worship which re-creates what actually happened in history. Through the re-presentation of these events in worship the triune God encounters us. And we respond to God through this ordered re-presentation.

Spontaneous response is therefore not related to changing the order, but to responding spontaneously to the order which re-presents God and his work in Jesus Christ. Let me give you an example of this from an actual service of worship in a Plymouth Brethren Church.

If you have ever worshiped at a Plymouth Brethren Church, you know that the sanctuary is very plain and simple, as is the service. As I entered, I noticed that all the people were seated in silence. Some were praying with heads bowed while others were reading Scripture, and some appeared to be meditating on the hymns. The atmosphere was one of quiet peace. A serenity pervaded the congregation. As I stood momentarily at the door, I felt a strong invitation to come and worship. The quiet bid me to enter the presence of God, to worship him. I slipped into a seat, bowed my head in prayer, and then read my Bible quietly as I continued to prepare for worship.

Soon, an elder rose to his feet and said, "We have come here to remember our Lord Jesus Christ and his work at Calvary. Let us continue our worship as we sing together, 'Lead Me to Calvary.' " As we sang, I felt the Calvary-event transported into that very assembly of people. We were responding to a call, a bidding by that hymn to come to Calvary. The chorus, "Lest I forget Gethsemane; lest I forget thine agony; lest I forget thy love for me; lead me to Calvary," brought me into the very presence of Jesus and reminded me that worship celebrates Christ.

After a few moments of silence, another elder stood and remarked how worship brings us up into the heavens before the very throne of God. He asked us to sing "The Holiest We Enter." Although I was unfamiliar with that particular hymn, the image of coming before the throne of God evoked my response to God in the heavens. While we sang, "Much incense is ascending before the eternal throne; God graciously is bending to hear each feeble groan; to all our prayers and praises Christ adds his sweet perfume; and love the center raises, these odors to consume," I experienced, like Isaiah, God seated on his throne and the whole earth was full of his glory.

I was still meditating on this experience when another elder stood to comment on the peace that floods our souls when we stand before our glorious God in worship of him. He invited us to sing, "Oh, the Peace Forever Flowing." And as we concluded with the words "Jesus Savior, we adore thee! Christ of God—Anointed Son! We confess thee, Lord of glory; Fruits of victory thou hast won!" I felt closure on my preparation for worship.

I had gone to Calvary, been lifted up into the heavens before the throne of God, and now experienced a flood of God's peace rush over my whole being. I was ready to hear the Word of God, to listen to him speak to me.

Allow me to step away from this service for just a moment and reflect on what happened. The order in this seemingly "spontaneous" church was really no different from that which I have experienced in many Episcopal, Lutheran, and Presbyterian churches. Sure, no one had a bulletin or a prayer book. Yet, the story told was the same. It was the story of Christ, focusing on his death and resurrection to the glory of the Father. And I was brought to the focal point of worship through the comments of the elders and the hymns. The service was true to the biblical and historic approach to worship I have been urging in this book. What had triggered my response was not something haphazardly put together, but the ordered, sequential presentation of the reason for my being at worship. As I sat there in worship, I wondered if we would now move into an exposition of the Word. Sure enough, we did.

After a short time of quiet to reflect on our preparation, an elder stood and read from Mark 15:15–41. He then elaborated on this passage, telling us about the suffering Christ went through on our behalf. We then sat in silence for several minutes thinking about the Scripture and his comments. Another person rose to his feet and said, "When we hear of Christ's death for us we are moved to a sense of peace with God and each other." He proceeded to read Ephesians 2:14–22 and expounded on the phrase, "He is our peace, who has made us both one, and has broken down the dividing wall of hostility by abolishing in his flesh the law of commandments and ordinances, that he might create in himself one new man in place of the two, so making peace, and might reconcile us both to God in one body through the cross, thereby bringing the hostility to an end."

As he ended his remarks, I felt the Word of God had been proclaimed, and that I had been moved to response and love through the reading, preaching, and hearing of the Word. Knowing that in the ancient tradition, as well as in the Reformation tradition of worship, a response of faith and prayer comes after the exposition of the Word, I wondered what would happen next. I bowed my head and began to respond to the Word in prayer, but I was not surprised when an elder stood and led the entire congregation in prayer. In an expressive and beautiful prayer, he recapitulated the entire service to that point and brought before God the needs of the congregation, of the world, and prayers of thanksgiving. I felt closure had been brought to this second part of the worship, and I wondered how God would direct the congregation into the worship of him at the Communion Table.

It wasn't long before another person stood and read Deuteronomy 5:2–3: "The Lord our God made a covenant with us in Horeb. Not with our fathers did the Lord make this covenant, but with us, who are all of us here alive this day." Then he said, "The experience of the Lord's Table can become a dull routine. I want to remind you today of Moses' words to Israel. He called to their attention that the covenant of God was with *us*. The original people who were brought through the Red Sea were dead. But the theophany continues. Sinai was a dynamic experience for all of Israel. It came through history and was to become alive for the next generation. The same is true for us. God is here, present now. His death, although it took place nearly two thousand years ago, is effective now for us. It is as though we were there. What was true for Israel is true for us. We are put in the Upper Room."

Almost immediately another elder said, "Let's sing 'Amidst Us Our Beloved Stands.'" We sang, "Amidst us our beloved stands, and bids us view his pierced hands; points to the wounded feet and side; blest emblems of the crucified," and I felt as though I were transported into the Upper Room in the presence of Jesus. I could hear him say, "See my hands and my feet, that it is I myself; handle me and see" (Luke 24:39).

Several elders stood and made brief comments. Then a prayer recounting the Last Supper and Christ's words of institution, together with prayers of thanksgiving, were said. Elders came with the bread and wine, and together with that congregation I entered into an intimate relationship with Christ. I bit the bread hard to claim all that it represented. I claimed Christ's healing and saving power as I swallowed the bread and drank from the cup of wine. In silence, as I sat there, I sensed the end had come to our worship. The order had brought me through the experience of preparation, hearing and responding to the Word, and entering into communion with God. Through eating and drinking at his Table, I was ready to leave, to go forth in peace to love and serve the Lord.

Again, after a few moments of quiet, an elder came forward and asked us to sing, "It Is Well with My Soul." I sang heartily, from deep within, for I had been brought through the event in history that did make it all well with my soul. I had experienced again the power of God searching me out, loving me, and claiming me for his own. My response was one of gratitude and praise. The elder made a few announcements and then closed the service in prayer.

I have given you this example, not because I am advocating this particular style of worship, or another for that matter, but because it is an excellent example of how the external form, the order of worship, leads, triggers, and evokes our response. Here, in what must definitely be called a nonliturgical church, that ancient sense of story, sequence, and order has been preserved in a spontaneous way. Such a service elicited my praise and worship of God.

Since God is speaking and acting in worship, response to God who speaks and acts is of great importance. In my response, I am once again saying yes to God. As with that initial response when I first heard the Word of God's love and grace, I again respond to him in faith and love.

This kind of response makes a difference. Worship is not something rote, mechanical, or intellectual. I do not worship because I've always done it. I don't worship because of peer pressure or for a better social standing in the community. I respond to God in worship because he makes a difference in my life.

Worship reminds me of my commitment to Christ. Worship calls me to love not only God with my whole heart, but my brother as myself. Therefore my response to God, who is present in worship, is the source of power for living. It sets my world in order. It determines my priorities in life. It puts me at peace with God, my neighbor, and my own life.

CHAPTER SEVEN

Return Worship to the People

Recently, I was talking with a devout Christian friend who was complaining about the worship of his church. I asked him, "What is it that offends you about the way worship is conducted in your church?" He looked me square in the eye and said, "It's the pastor-centered service. The pastor does everything—leads the service, reads the Scripture, prays, and preaches. What I want is a service where the gifts of all God's people are expressed."

I have found an increasing desire among Evangelicals to return worship to the people. Pastor Bob Harvey told me that one of the major concerns of his congregation is how to go about increasing participation in worship. For example, Alva Steffler, who is a member of the Bethel Presbyterian Church where Bob Harvey is pastor, said, "We're going back to the biblical idea of everyone in the church being able to exercise his or her gifts. I feel really good about offering my gifts to the church."

In spite of the rising tide of lay participation in worship, barriers still exist. Pastor Loren McLean feels lay people still tend to set the pastor on a pedestal: "We are looked on as professionals . . . the ones who have some kind of mysterious power so that God speaks through us and not through other people. It's like the power of the mystic God that comes from the medieval age. Many people hold that view subconsciously. When I ask people to participate in worship, to pray or read, their first impulse is to back away and say, 'You shouldn't be asking me to do that.' It's not because they're lazy or think I'm trying to get out of work. They really believe that a minister is in a different relationship to God than they are. Actually, we claim to believe in the priesthood of all believers, but we don't practice it." With this thought in mind, let's now look at some ideas to help restore congregational participation in the worship experience.

CORPORATE CONGREGATIONAL PARTICIPATION

For our purposes here, let's define congregational participation as worship which involves the action of everyone simultaneously. But it seems to me that congregational action cannot occur without two very basic ingredients: the congregation must understand what they are doing, and they must intend to make the responses that are part of worship. *Worship is a verb.*

I have discovered that worship is best understood when it carries the worshiper through a sequence of related events such as: (1) Preparation to worship, (2) reading and preaching the Word, (3) Holy Communion, and (4) Dismissal. In this sequence, the story of our coming to God—of hearing him speak, of entering into communion with him, and of being sent forth—is the order of worship (see chapter 3, "The Order of Worship").

In large measure this sequence for worship has been lost in many evangelical churches today. But I want now to suggest several practical reasons why this pattern which reflects Acts 2:42 should be restored.

A Meeting between God and His People

The first reason for restoring the story sequence of Preparation, Word, Table, and Dismissal as a pattern for worship is that worship is a meeting between God and his people. Like all other meetings between two or more people, a certain amount of form is necessary.

For example, when we meet a friend or neighbor, we go through a form we have used many times. We say, "Hello . . . How are you? . . . How is the family? . . . Are you still on the job?" And usually we shake hands or embrace as a sign of our relationship with that person.

A similar set of rituals surrounds our departure from friends or relatives. But they don't grow old or lose their meaning merely because they are repeated over and over again. The rituals we use in our social relationships are extremely important, as are the forms we use in worship. They are the outward means through which our inward and heartfelt praise of God are communicated.

For this reason, I don't believe that the forms of our traditional worship should be discarded as useless relics of the past. Those who advocate a so-called creative worship designed to give the congregation a new spiritual high every week soon discover that this is not only impossible but impractical. God has already established the structural ingredients needed in a meeting with him, and we cannot improve on these forms. We simply need to understand what they are and practice them in faith, believing that we really are meeting God in his Word and through his Table.

To help us understand more clearly, we need to examine the basic implication of worship as a meeting between God and his people. By wrestling with this matter in my own pilgrimage, I have come to see that it is in the worship experience that our relationship to God is established and sustained. For example, the purpose of the meeting between God and the Hebrews at Mt. Sinai was clearly to establish a relationship with them (see Exod. 24:1–8). In this dramatic confrontation, God entered into a covenantal agreement with Israel—they became his people and he became their God. Moses later commented on this relationship by reminding the people of Israel,

"You are a people holy to the Lord your God; the Lord your God has chosen you to be a people for his own possession, out of all the peoples that are on the face of the earth" (Deut. 7:6). Actually, their redemption was certified in the Exodus-event, but it was at Sinai that the relationship between God and Israel became a reality.

Christian worship is like Hebrew worship. In worship God renews his covenant with us. In worship our relationship to God is deepened and strengthened when the order itself represents God's speaking to us and God's saving us through the life, death, and resurrection of his Son. The order brings that ancient event into our experience and causes, by the power of the Holy Spirit, a meeting to take place between God and us.

Let me give you an example from my own experience. When I participate in public worship, I ask God to let my imagination run free. I picture myself meeting God personally. As I prepare to worship, I envision him seated on the throne and allow the words of the hymn or the prayer to actually bring me before God Almighty. Then I confess my sin and hear him speak words of forgiveness to me. As I allow my imagination to work in the Preparation, the Word, the Communion, and the Dismissal, I feel that I am participating in something that is actually happening. Worship is not just going on outside of me or around me, but within me.

The point of this illustration is to show that worship is a meeting with God. We stand before him and respond to his great glory; we hear him speak and respond to what he says; we become the recipients of his saving deed through the symbols of bread and wine, and we respond; we hear him send us forth and our response continues in the world.

Worship that isn't a meeting with God doesn't provide the appropriate setting in which an interaction with God may take place. Worship that tells a story and carries us through a sequence not only inspires our response, but establishes a point of meeting between God and us so that we can experience God's speaking and acting, as well as our responding and interacting with him. In this way the order of our worship serves our meeting with God.

The Priesthood of All Believers

Next, another practical reason for restoring the biblical sequence of Preparation, Word, Table, and Dismissal is that it makes possible the recovery of the priesthood of all believers. Medieval and pre-Reformation worship was clergy-centered—the congregation merely watched and observed; they were spectators, not participants. However, in the sixteenth century, the Reformers insisted on a form of worship that was distinctly congregational—a worship done *by the people.* But now, four centuries later, much of our modern worship has drifted back into the pattern of the medieval church. It seems very strange to me that the biblical principle of the priesthood of all believers, which was the hallmark of Reformation Christianity, has now been lost in so much of our Protestant worship.

But, a remedy, I believe, for the performer/audience psychology that we have created in our services is the radical rediscovery of the principle of the priesthood of all believers—a principle that encourages everyone to become involved in a participating manner in offering the worship of praise and thanksgiving to the Father.

Pastor friends of mine tell me that the audience mentality of many Protestant churches is the greatest barrier to the recovery of the involvement of all God's people in worship. We are, I fear, conditioned by the television set to the state of being uninvolved. We want to watch someone else perform. We want to be entertained. We seem to prefer not lifting a finger to active participation.

Recently, I was talking to a colleague of mine who

left his church to join another. I asked, "Why did you leave?"

"Bob," he answered, "I've simply had it up to my ears with a worship that's directed toward me. The sermon, the songs, even the special music is almost always person-centered. My wife and I have sensed a growing dissatisfaction with this kind of worship for a long time. We are tired of sitting and having somebody else do something for us. We've recently concluded that church for us has been little more than being in the presence of nice people. Although we love these people, we want more than that."

With these thoughts in mind, my colleague had chosen a church that puts a high priority on a God-centered worship and the involvement of the people. Knowing this, I asked, "How's the new church going?"

He answered me with a sense of enthusiasm and a smile that spread across his entire face. "It's a profound experience of worship."

"Why?" I asked.

"Because I feel drawn up in the presence of God and sent back into the world with a sense of inner refreshment and satisfaction." Then he added, "You know, I just love to be at worship. I can't live without it. What happens on Sunday morning is something that I'm doing too. And it spills over into my whole week."

Recovering the priesthood of all believers does not mean asking a few people to do something during worship. It means that everyone becomes so involved in worship that the whole community worships together as a body.

Let me give you an example of something that happened to me in church. A woman sitting behind me interacted with everything that was happening in the service in such a way that I was moved to a deeper experience of meeting the Lord through her response. As the Word was being read she softly whispered, "Yes, yes, oh yes,

that's true." As the preacher spoke she responded again
with the words, "Yes, oh yes," a number of times. Her
involvement was intense, warm, and full of feeling. She
was meeting with God, hearing him speak, and responding to him. I wanted to go up to her after church and
thank her, because her response assisted me in my meeting with God. But I didn't. I now wish I had.

That woman was exercising her right in the priesthood
of all believers to be directly involved in the whole story
of worship. She was alert to what was happening. And
this is the kind of aliveness we want to restore to our
worship.

Order and Freedom

A third reason for maintaining the biblical sequence
of Preparation, Word, Table, and Dismissal as a pattern
for spiritual renewal is that this structure provides a context in which the struggle between order and freedom
can take place authentically.

Not long ago, I went to a church where the order of
worship told and acted out the story. The bulletin indicated that we would be prepared to meet God, hear him
speak, commune with him, and be sent forth. Each part
was in the right sequence. But the service was dead and
dull. The people seemed listless, uninvolved, uncaring,
and nonintentional. There was no enthusiasm, no sense
of the power and presence of the Holy Spirit. Every action
seemed rote, and mechanical. There was no spontaneity,
no sense of interaction, and very little communication
going on. In this church the order was seen as an end
in itself. The service, therefore, was stifling; and it had
the effect of smothering the spirit of freedom.

I had a very different experience in another church
where I was speaking only a few weeks later. In this
second church, there was no order at all. The minister
started the service by asking for some hymns. After we

sang, Scripture was read, a solo was sung, the money was collected, we sang again, I was introduced to speak, we sang another hymn, and the meeting was closed with prayer. There seemed to be no rhyme or reason to the order of worship. It was chaotic and unfulfilling for me. I even felt upset inside. The focal point and purpose of the whole service had been my sermon. Nothing else really seemed to matter. Nevertheless, everyone seemed to have a good time. They had responded with favorite hymns, sung lustily, often laughed, and appeared to have good camaraderie. But is that what worship is about?

Now the question we face is this: How can we, and the church, experience a form of worship that is truly free, yet is characterized by order? This, I believe, is a question that must always be in our minds. It is an issue which lies at the heart of a lively and active worship. Order without freedom may become mere unthinking ritual. On the other hand, freedom without order may become equally unthinking and even chaotic. But the order and style of worship which we're talking about here, and which I believe is biblical, is one that re-enacts the Gospel story.

The freedom I urge is that of a lively faith, an active and engaging commitment to what is being done, a freedom to be spontaneous within the context of order. Since order is the symbol of God's speaking and acting in the midst of his church, there can be no justification for passive worshipers who simply sit and soak it all in. Certainly, as we have seen, passive worship cannot be justified on the grounds of Scripture, theology, or history. For this reason, it is a matter of utmost urgency that the church break through the obstacle of a passive worship. And it is important that we see in worship renewal a rediscovery of a structure through which Christ is faithfully presented and rediscovered, a worship that is free and intentional. To help us understand what is involved we will now move to an examination of that structure and to some specific suggestions that will encourage corporate and individual participation from the heart.

SUGGESTIONS FOR CORPORATE AND INDIVIDUAL PARTICIPATION

We have seen that the pastor and other leaders of worship are not merely performers. Instead, they are leaders in a corporate drama of Christ's living, dying, and rising again. For this reason, worship is not a one-way monologue between the leader and the congregation, but a dialogue between them.

Worship as Dialogue

Since worship is a dialogue, we need to find ways to break away from our passive roles as worshipers and recover an interaction between the worship leader and the congregation. One way to do this is to restore the use of the *Salutation*, the *Amen*, the *Thanks be to God*, and the *Alleluia*. These acclamations are all rooted in the Bible and, as we'll discuss shortly, have been used in the worship of the church.

The Salutation engages the entire congregation in prayer. It is rooted in an ancient Hebrew greeting first found in Ruth 2:4 and became part of worship in the early church. In many churches the minister stretches his arms forward in a gesture of openness toward God and invites the congregation to prayer by saying, "The Lord be with you." If the congregation does not answer, worship may not proceed. But when the congregation responds, "And also with you," permission has been granted to pray.

Because the prayer that is being said represents the entire congregation it is concluded by a congregational amen. The "Amen," which is of Hebrew derivation, was used in the early church (see 1 Cor. 14:16). It means "so be it." I tell my college students "If I pray, 'Lord grant each member of this class an "A," ' you would certainly add your 'Amen' to that prayer." Since one person is praying for all the people, representing them, the "Amen" should not be neglected. It connotes involvement and brings an end to the prayer, while providing a spiritual transition to the next part of the unfolding worship drama.

The acclamation, "Thanks be to God" is related to the sense expressed in 2 Cor. 4:15. Here Paul states, "As grace extends to more and more people, it may increase thanksgiving, to the glory of God." This statement of thanksgiving may come spontaneously throughout the service as a response to testimonials, affirmations of faith, or other declarations of God's grace. Traditionally, it occurs after the reading of Scripture. Upon completing the reading, the reader may say, "This is the Word of the Lord." Then the congregation may respond with an enthusiastic "Thanks be to God." For me, one of the most surprising instances of this heartfelt thanks occurred during my visit to the Church of the Holy Trinity in Russia. At the conclusion of the priest's sermon, the entire congregation shouted in one voice, "Pasiba." It was like an electric response. I turned to my translator and said, "What's that?" It means, "Thank you," he said. I thought to myself, "No wonder it was said with such enthusiasm. These people who can't have the Word of God shout thank you when they hear this Word of grace." And I was ashamed that I took the Word of God which is so readily available to me for granted.

Another acclamation which ought to be restored in our worship is the "Alleluia." It is a Hebrew word derived from *hallelui* (the imperative of hillel, *to praise*) and *Jah* (an abbreviation of Jahue, *God*). Thus it means "praise be to God." It is an acclamation of praise frequently used in the New Testament (see Rev. 19:1, 3, 4, 6), and used in the earliest Christian services of worship. It is reported that ancient Christians loved to sing the "Alleluia" so much that on occasion they would sing the phrase for twenty or thirty minutes. Sometimes they had to be stopped so the service could go on.

I have personally experienced the power of this phrase on a number of occasions. In my church we sing the "Alleluia" before the reading of the Gospel. I always feel carried up into the heavens and sense that I am standing in the very presence of Christ who is now addressing me. But for me, the most special time to sing the "Alleluia" is on Easter Sunday. As the entire congregation joins in "Alleluia, Sing to Jesus," that word penetrates into the center of my being and creates within me an outpouring of praise. I feel touched by the Holy Spirit and released by his power to truly experience a "praise be to God!"

The responses I have mentioned above are short and conducive to the sense of an immediate heartfelt response. Long responses should be avoided. They require reading, and they tend to be rational and discursive rather than performative and symbolic.

Because these responses are biblical and attested to in history, it is important that passive congregations recover them. They have the effect of getting people involved in the action. They give life to the structure, feed faith in the worshiper, and create a sense of unity and oneness among the members of the body of Christ.

In addition to these acclamations, it is quite important to get people involved on an individual basis. Each person acting as a minister may indeed minister to the body through his or her particular gift.

The description of New Testament worship given by Paul in 1 Corinthians 12–14 is full of congregational action. Paul's emphasis is on the church as a body. To each one, he says, "is given the manifestation of the spirit for the common good" (1 Cor. 12:7). He then indicates that when God's people come together to worship, each one comes with "a hymn, a lesson, a revelation, a tongue, or an interpretation. Let all things be done for edification" (1 Cor. 14:26).

The impression given by Paul is that worship in Corinth was not only very active, but slightly disorganized. Consequently, he ends his admonition by saying, "All things should be done decently and in order" (1 Cor. 14:40).

An Example

In order to give you a more complete sense of a worship service that contains the fixed order of Preparation, Word, Table, and Dismissal, together with a free and spontaneous congregational response, I will give you an example. I could illustrate this combination of order and freedom from many experiences, but I have chosen a service of worship developed by my students in a class on worship.

In this particular class, I divide the students into groups and require each group to develop an authentic worship service from a particular period. This year's students have developed an ancient Jewish service, a third-century service, a sixteenth-century Calvinist service, an eighteenth-century Wesleyan service, and three model contemporary services. As we perform these services and discuss them, we seek to draw from the rich resources they provide in the development of a service of worship for today. A few weeks ago we did a third-century service of worship. I want to explain what we did to give you an idea of the kind of personal involvement that was experienced in the ancient church.

The students decided to have the service in the rotunda of the Billy Graham Museum which is located in the Graham Center at Wheaton College. The group chose the rotunda because I had instructed them to have the worship service in a setting that was architecturally reminiscent of the era. They felt, I think appropriately, that this rotunda is reminiscent of the catacombs.

The rotunda is very striking. It is, as I stated, the entrance to the Museum on Evangelism. It is large, about 78 feet in circumference, with a ceiling about 25 feet high. The floor is covered in deep black carpeting, and the walls are black as well. The black is accented by a contrasting white ceiling and a round white marble plaque centered in the floor and inscribed with the words, "I am the light of the world. Whoever follows me will never walk in darkness, but will have the light of life." A perpetual beam of light from the ceiling shines down on the plaque and casts its rays across the black floor and walls. As you look, you will see another contrast to the black—nine, fifteen-foot-long, off-white banners with the likeness of some of the great evangelists of the church sewn onto each in multiple colors. We are surrounded by Paul, Justin Martyr, Gregory the Great, Francis of Assisi, John Wycliffe, Martin Luther, Blaise Paschal, Jonathan Edwards, and Oswald Chambers. In addition, on the white ceiling, hidden machines flash in slow succession about 120 different names of Jesus. Whenever I stand in the rotunda, I sense the struggle between good and evil, the victory of Christ over the powers of darkness, and the great cloud of witnesses throughout history who have preached Christ. The students made a good choice when they selected the rotunda as a place to worship.

Sometimes in the ancient church Christians gathered outside their meeting place and then marched together into the place of worship as a sign of entrance into the presence of Christ. The students chose to follow this practice. We were told to enter quietly and prayerfully and remain standing as we waited for the service to begin. As I stood there, I looked at the simple Communion Table that symbolized my Lord's death and resurrection, and I asked God to receive my worship as an act of thanksgiving to him.

The worship leader began the service by saying, "Praise ye the Lord who is to be praised"; and we all responded, "Praise ye the Lord who is to be praised forever and ever." In this brief dialogue, which is Jewish in origin, we acknowledged that we had come together to praise God.

The leader then led us in a prayer of invocation. "The Lord be with you," he cried; and we all responded, "And also with you." After his spontaneous prayer invoking God's presence in our worship, we all responded with "Amen."

The dialogue continued as we were brought before the throne of God through the "Gloria in Excelsis Deo." A small choir of students sang, "Lord God, Heavenly King, Almighty God and Father"; and we responded with "Glory to God in the highest and peace to his people on earth." This antiphonal song continued as they sang, "We worship you; we give you thanks; we praise you for your glory"; and, again, we sang the refrain. Then the choir, their voices becoming stronger, sang, "Lord Jesus Christ, only Son of the Father, Lord God, Lamb of God, you take away the sin of the world, have mercy upon us; you are seated at the right hand of the Father, receive our prayer." Again we sang the refrain. Finally, the climax of this glorious ancient hymn was reached as the choir sang, "For you alone are the Holy One, you alone are the Lord, you alone are the Most High, Jesus Christ, with the Holy Spirit, in the glory of God the Father"; and we, more loudly and clearly now, as though to join with the heavenly Host and those whose likeness was gathered around us, sang lustily, "Glory to God in the highest, and peace to his people on earth."

As we were standing there in the very presence of the God whom we had proclaimed as "alone the Lord, alone the Most High," the leader asked us to confess our sins. After a short while he declared the words of forgiveness. A sense of peace flooded my soul. I felt prepared now to hear the Word of the Lord.

Before taking you into the Word, however, I want to reflect on the nature of dialogue in the Preparation. I felt involved in what was going on. It wasn't something being done to me or for me. Rather, I was involved in the action. True, it could have been rote and mechanical, but my intention to worship coupled with the faith and intention of the body gathered for worship prevented this preparation from being a mere recital of words. Together we were involved in an experience of worship that felt like a conversation and exchange with God himself in the presence of the saints.

The overall purpose of the Preparation is not only to begin the service of worship, but to help us, as the people of God, be formed into a distinct community of worshiping people. We need time to collect ourselves, to settle down inwardly, to be reminded of who God is, who we are, and why we have gathered. In other words, the mood for worship must be established.

The mood of the Preparation is one of quiet humility and openness before God. It is not a time for hilarity or jokes or visiting. It is more appropriate to be pensive, meditative, and low key. We should experience a longing to be in the presence of the Lord, and to hear God's word of forgiveness and acceptance. The result of the Preparation is a readiness to hear the Word of the Lord.

Although there is no set or prescribed way in which the Preparation *must* be done, the order of events does have an inner unfolding, a dynamic of its own, which carries the worshipers through a series of actions culminating in the sense of forgiveness. But the order in no way forces a formal service on those who desire greater informality. The same sense of preparation may be accomplished through an informal approach.

For example, each month Pastor Bob Harvey has a different elder involved in the planning and leading of the Preparation. "We ask each person to lead the Preparation as he or she sees fit. It's his responsibility to choose the expression of God's law, to lead in prayer, to ask others to pray, to choose the hymn, and to announce the declaration of pardon."

While congregational involvement is a high priority, it should not be turned into a show nor should a carnival atmosphere be created. All that is done and all who are involved should exude a joyful seriousness before the Lord, and thus assist the Spirit in preparing the people to hear the Word of God.

Let's return to our third-century service in the rotunda. Now that we had been led in the preparation of our hearts to worship, we were ready to hear God speak to us through the Word read and preached. The students chose Scripture readings from the Old Testament, the Epistles, and the Gospel. These readings were interspersed with the singing of psalms, and at the end of each reading the reader said, "The Word of the Lord," to which we all responded, "Thanks be to God."

This emphasis on Scripture reading is authentic in respect to the ancient tradition. During the third century it was the custom to read lengthy portions of Scriptures, even whole books at a time. Since individuals and families did not have Bibles, the only opportunity they had to hear the Word of God was in the assembly of worship. We read less Scripture in worship today because people have their own Bibles. However, the universal practice is to read, as my students did, at least three passages with psalms.

The overall purpose for the reading of the Word is to let God speak. It is not, as some think, the time for educating the people, for long tedious exegetical sermons, or an evangelistic appeal. It is principally an address from God to the congregation that is expressed through reading and preaching his Word and is followed by an appropriate response from the people.

In the ancient church, Scriptures were often sung antiphonally. Today we may want to recover that practice or find other ways to increase the involvement of the people in the scriptural portion of our worship. Many churches have started a lay readers' group or a drama group whose special gift is that of reading or acting out Scripture portions.

Once again, allow me to digress from the service for

a moment and offer a few examples from personal inter-
views and from my own experience in worship that illustrate some of the suggestions I have made for
congregational involvement in the Word.

Pastor Ames Broen described a Scripture reading in
which the same passage was read twice. After the first
reading, which had been done in the usual manner, the
Scripture was read again with another voice overlaying
it with related contemporary comments from a book urging people to social involvement in today's world. "This
had the effect of bringing realism into the text. It took
it from another world and placed it squarely in the context of the congregation's contemporary life in today's
world," said Broen.

Pastor Neil Garrabrant has occasionally involved other
informed people in the sermon itself. For example, one
of his members is a history buff and somewhat of a sleuth
when it comes to finding out the background and origin
of things. Garrabrant has used him on special occasions
to dig out the background of a passage. The historian
presents his findings as part of the sermon, usually in
the beginning as a preface to the proclamation. Because
people understand the historical context, its relevance
to their situation in the world becomes more obvious.

Now let's return to the third-century service. After the
Scriptures were read, the student worship leaders led
us in a time of response to the Word. The first response
was a sermon that simply commented on the scriptural
text. In many of our churches today, sermons seem unre-
lated to the text. In the early church, however, the comments were simple and direct implications and applica-
tions from the text, designed to help the Christian be a
better follower of Jesus. It is not unreasonable to assume
that in the smaller and less formal Christian communities
of the ancient church discussion and application of the
text may have followed the sermon.

Today, a number of ministers are attempting to get
their people more involved in the Scripture through di-

rect response to the Word that is read and preached. Pastor Henry Jauhiainen allows for a reflective time after the sermon and encourages response from the people. People stand and make short comments describing how the Scripture spoke to them and met their needs. Pastor Jauhiainen says, "I've had to instruct my people not to give us a second sermon, but a simple response. This time of sharing has become a vital part of our worship."

When David Mains was pastor of Circle Church in Chicago, he occasionally announced the sermon topic for the following week and asked people to meditate on the topic and prepare a short response. He scheduled ten minutes for response, allowing one minute for each person. One woman told him, "It made my whole week, just planning what I was going to say." In other churches the response to the Word is carried over into a forum at the conclusion of the service.

As we have seen, there are a variety of ways we can respond to the Word. But, no matter how it is accomplished, congregational response to the Word is a very important means of sealing the Word in this heart and life.

A second form of response is prayer. As in the early church, the student leaders led us in prayer after we had responded to the Word. Again, the placement of prayer after the Word is crucial. We have been brought into the very presence of God. In his presence, we have waited to hear him speak before laying our concerns before him. We have not blurted out our cares and concerns without paying attention to what he has to say. But now that he has spoken to us through his Word, what better time is there to take before him our collective and individual concerns? Now is the time for petition: prayers for the local people of God and their needs, prayers for the whole church worldwide, and prayers for the needs of the world.

In the ancient church pastoral prayer was nonexistent. Prayer belonged to the people and arose out of the congregation. If our interest is rediscovering traditional worship, there are many ways prayer may be given back to people in a contemporary setting. For example, pastor Bob Harvey returns prayer to the congregation by asking four or five people to offer prayers of intercession from within the congregation. I have often led congregational prayer by announcing areas of prayer. I'll say, "Let us pray for the needs of this congregation—for those who are sick, and those in need of the guidance of the Holy Spirit." After a short season of prayer I'll say, "Let's pray for the needs of the world—for the hungry, the needy, and the oppressed," and so on until all the areas of prayer have been covered. Usually, I ask for spoken responses. Some will pray out loud. But others will pray quietly. On occasion, if it seems most appropriate, all prayers may be done in silence or a quiet whisper.

One of my most memorable experiences in congregational prayer occurred in Boston recently. I was walking downtown and passed an Episcopal church bearing the sign, "Noon Prayer in the Chapel." I entered the church and knelt with the person who was to lead the noon prayer service. Since I was the only one there, I was a little uncertain what was going to happen. But I picked up the prayer book and read the responses as would an entire congregation. When it came time for the prayers of intercession, I noticed the leader had a fairly large stack of index cards in her hand. We knelt and she began to read the requests: "A new van is needed for missionaries in Burma, India. Let us pray to the Lord." And I answered to this request and all others, "Lord, hear our prayer." I felt deeply involved in these prayers and in that whole service. It was truly a dialogic experience. I have used this same pattern of prayer in larger congregations where it would be awkward or less convenient to call upon the people for individual prayers. These, and

other ways, may help us break through the passive practice of prayer to a more increased involvement of God's
people in bringing their petitions before the Lord.

In the early church it was appropriate to offer the kiss
of peace after the prayers. True to early church practice,
my students asked us all to stand after the prayers and,
before extending the kiss of peace, offered us a brief explanation. "In the early church," one of the students said,
"it was the custom to pass the peace of Christ. Let me
explain what it is." She then proceeded to tell us how
the kiss of peace was a gesture signifying that we are
at peace with God and with our neighbors. Because God
has reconciled us to the Father through Jesus Christ, we
ought to be reconciled to each other. Paul himself, we
were told, had instructed the believers to greet each
other with a similar Christian salutation (see Rom. 16:15;
1 Cor. 16:20; 2 Cor. 13:12; 1 Thess. 5:26; and 1 Pet. 5:14).
"For the early Christians," she said, "this gesture had
tremendous meaning. Many were under pressure in their
jobs, and the lives of some were threatened because of
their faith. So to have the peace of God passed to them
was an encouragement in their Christian life." She urged
us to pass the peace with a handshake or an embrace,
and with a real sense of warmth and love, saying, "The
peace of the Lord be with you." In this action—this response to the word of reconciliation—I felt a real kinship
with the students in that class. They were more than
my students, they were my brothers and sisters in Christ;
they were fellow travelers in the Christian pilgrimage
of faith.

In the ancient church the kiss of peace marked the
end of the service of the Word and the beginning of
the service of the Communion Table. Again, true to the
ancient church, the students planned the Communion
around the fourfold action at the Last Supper—the taking,
blessing, breaking, and giving.

During the taking, the bread and wine were brought

to the Table and an offering for the needy was collected. It was announced to us by the worship leader that the money collected would be given to a needy family in the college community. Then we were invited to bring our offering to the Table and put it into the plate. As we left our offerings, the bread and wine were placed on the table. I liked this approach because it gave me an opportunity to be involved. I sensed that I was giving something of myself, something of my work and earnings, which helped me relate to the self-giving of Christ symbolized by the bread and wine.

After we had brought our gifts and the elements of bread and wine to the Table, the ordained graduate student who was leading this part of our worship service stretched forth his hands in an upward gesture and said, "Lift up your hearts." We responded with, "We lift them up to the Lord," to which he said, "Let us give thanks to the Lord." We responded, "It is meet and right."

These are the opening words of the earliest Communion prayer known in the Christian church. They were written by Hippolytus, a minister in the church at Rome in 220 A.D. I felt involved by the words and gesture. I had been called upon to lift up my heart to the Lord, and by word of mouth and intention of my heart I responded to the call.

The celebrant continued with the prayer handed down from the early church: "We give thee thanks, O God, through thy beloved servant Jesus Christ, whom at the end of time thou didst send to us a Savior and Redeemer and the Messenger of my council." In these words he stated the reason for our being there. It was to celebrate Jesus Christ as Savior of the world. Since this is the same reason why the angels and archangels, the prophets and apostles, and the martyrs and saints who have gone before us worship Jesus, the ancient church adopted the custom of singing the heavenly song recorded in Revelation 4:8. As we stood there in the rotunda, but, as it were, now lifted into the very presence of God, a student sang in a high, clear voice, "Holy, Holy, Holy, Lord of Sabaoth, heaven and earth are full of your glory. Hosanna in the highest. Blessed is he who comes in the name of the Lord. Hosanna in the highest." I felt the presence of God penetrate into my very being and fill my whole body with a sense of exultant joy.

We dropped to our knees as instructed and stretched our arms forward with palms directed upward as a symbol of receptivity for the Holy Spirit. Then the celebrant continued with the prayer from Hippolytus:

> Who is thy word, inseparable from thee; through whom thou didst make all things and in whom thou art well pleased.
> Whom thou didst send from heaven into the womb of the virgin, and who, dwelling within her, was made flesh, and was manifested as thy Son, being born of the Holy Spirit and the virgin.
> Who, fulfilling thy will, and winning for himself a holy people, spread out his hands when he came to suffer, that by his death he might set them free who believed on thee.
> Who, when he was betrayed to his willing death, that he might bring to nought death, and break the bonds of the devil, and tread hell under foot, and give light to the righteous, and set up a boundary post, and manifest his resurrection, taking bread and giving thanks to thee said . . .

As these words of the Gospel were spoken, the celebrant took the bread and lifted it for us to see, and then lifted the cup as well. In that instant, I not only heard the Gospel, I also saw the Gospel with my own eyes, and I continued to hear the Gospel in the breaking of the bread. The celebrant continued his prayer:

> Having in memory, therefore, his death and resurrection, we offer to thee the bread and the cup, yielding thee thanks, because thou hast counted us worthy to stand before thee and to minister to thee.

As he spoke these words, I was reminded that my offering of praise and thanksgiving to God is actually as these words say, "a ministry to thee." "God," I said to myself, "loves to be worshiped. And he has given me this wonderful privilege to bless his holy name, to magnify and glorify him." I felt overwhelmed by the awesome privilege which was mine. The prayer continued:

> And we pray thee that thou wouldst send thy Holy Spirit upon the offerings of thy Holy Church; that thou gathering them into one . . .

I felt that oneness with my students, with St. Paul, Justin Martyr, Martin Luther, Oswald Chambers, and others who were there or represented in that worshiping community. I knew I was not alone, that I belonged to a great body of people, that I was "surrounded by so great a cloud of witnesses" (Heb. 12:1).

> Grant to all thy saints who partake to be filled with the Holy Spirit, that their faith may be confirmed in truth, that we may praise and glorify thee, through thy servant Jesus Christ, through whom be to thee glory and honour, with the Holy Spirit in the holy church, both now and always, and world without end. Amen.

At the conclusion of the prayer we were invited to stand, walk to the Table, stretch out our hands, and receive the bread with the words "The Body of Christ, the Bread of Heaven," and to lift the cup to our mouths and drink with the words "The Blood of Christ, the Cup of Salvation." As I took these elements I said, "Amen," as was the custom in the early church. I liked standing, walking, and receiving in this manner because I felt I was putting my yes to Christ's death and resurrection for me, not only by my words, but also by my bodily action.

This same service of worship is used in many churches

today with some adaptations. In the third century when Hippolytus wrote it, he suggested it be used as a guide in worship. If one takes the time to examine it, it becomes readily apparent that it re-enacts the Gospel by word and asks the worshiper to act out once again his or her response of faith. I liked the simple and direct approach of this service, and felt it drew me into the action and made me a willing participant of the celebration of Christ's death and resurrection.

The internal development of worship is apparent in this account of the Table. The rhythm and movement of Communion is highly symbolic of the spiritual life itself. By bringing the bread and wine to the Table, we bring ourselves before the Lord. He takes that bread and wine which represent the fruit of our labor and returns it to us as the body and blood of his Son, shed for us. We bless him for so great a salvation, and yet we join in the breaking of that body because of our own sin. But bread and wine, these elements of creation, become the symbols of re-creation. For his body broken for us and his blood spilt for us are the signs of renewal and restoration. Thus, we are ministered to by the bread and wine, enabling us in turn to minister to the needs of others. In this way we are prepared for the Dismissal and our life in the world.

In the early church the Dismissal was very brief and to the point. Since the service was over, all that was left to do was to send the people forth with a blessing. In our college class service, we received the benediction and then, as we had come in, we recessed together. This corporate recession gave me the feeling that we were being sent forth into the world to serve the Lord. It left me with something more than, "The service is over; let's go home." I have found many pastors today are becoming more concerned about the sense of response that extends into the world from worship, and rightly so. They want their people to feel sent.

For example, Pastor Henry Jauhiainen has a helpful and, I believe, biblical idea of the Dismissal. "Worship," he says, "cannot be an end in itself. Every service is followed by a comma instead of a period. We worship as pilgrims. Worship enables us to carry on in a journey of hope." Another insight from Jauhiainen is that in worship we are acting together as priests not only within the body of Christ but beyond to the world. He says, "Since we pray for those who don't yet praise God, we have a priesthood on their behalf. This puts a missionary theology into our worship, so when we go forth we should go with a sense of our mission."

The Dismissal ought to convey this message in word and action. The minister may bless the congregation by proclaiming its calling in life, and this may be followed by the benediction and a hymn of triumph and joy which conveys the sense of being sent forth in the victory of Christ over sin, death, and the dominion of evil. The mood is that of joy, triumph, zeal, dedication, and festivity.

In this chapter my concern has been to suggest that we return worship to the people. Worship should be, I believe, a congregational action which involves the community as a whole and engages all the people in an active response to the fixed order of Preparation, Word, Table, and Dismissal.

I believe with all my heart that we evangelical people really want to worship. I believe we want to break the tradition of a nonactive, passive, and routine worship. As we continue to recover the dialogic nature of worship, and as we learn to increase our participation individually and collectively, our churches will become stronger. They will, I believe, be characterized by a stronger sense of community, and our mission to the world will be strengthened. So let's return worship to the people.

CHAPTER EIGHT

All Creation Joins in Worship

Last summer I attended a wedding in a small midwestern town. The church in which the wedding was held was a typical evangelical church—one deeply concerned about the Gospel, prayer, Bible study, and its witness in the community.

As I entered the sanctuary, I noticed the bulletins for the next day (Sunday) on a nearby table. Being a bulletin collector of sorts, I picked one up to look through as I sat waiting for the wedding festivities to begin.

Boldly pictured on its front cover, with no apology to the church or to the events it celebrates in worship, was the classic World War II snapshot of the American soldiers lifting the flag into position over Iwo Jima. Instantly, the image reminded me of the many soldiers who had given their lives to secure my freedom.

Curious about how this picture related to Sunday's worship, I opened the bulletin and glanced at the order of service. It was to be a memorial service for those lost in battle. And each element of worship—the hymns, the Scripture readings, the special music, and the sermon—had been adapted for a celebration of Memorial Day, a national holiday.

As I sat there wondering about the appropriateness of turning morning worship into a celebration of our national heritage, my mind drifted back to a conversation I had with Neil Garrabrant. I had spoken with Pastor Neil shortly after Mother's Day, and we talked about the idea of a sacred view of time. He made a comment that I'll probably never forget. "You know, Bob, last week we celebrated Mother's Day in our church. Everything in the service was geared toward honoring mothers. Our hymns, Scripture, sermon, and special music assisted us in the celebration of motherhood. When I got home, I sat down and started to think about that service. And I said to myself, 'We didn't worship God today; we were worshiping motherhood.'" He looked down at his books piled on his desk and paused as though the whole experience was running through his mind again. Then he looked up at me and with a touch of sadness in his eye and a tremor in his voice said, "You know, Bob, I don't think that service was real worship."

I thought for a moment about Neil's comments. Then I recalled the first principle of worship: *Worship celebrates Christ.* I had to agree with my friend.

I am deeply concerned that Evangelicals who are alarmed over the pervasiveness of secularism in our schools, on television, and in contemporary music seem unaware of a similar trend in our churches. Often, we operate with a secular calendar in mind, adjusting our schedules according to the academic calendar and the national calendar of holidays. As I have illustrated, even in our services we celebrate Boy Scouts' Day, Girl Scouts' Day, Mother's Day, Father's Day, and the like. But few evangelical churches follow the Christian calendar of Advent, Christmas, Epiphany, Lent, Holy Week, Easter, Pentecost, and Trinity season except on a few special days such as Christmas and Easter.

Recently I was giving a lecture on "The Theology of Time" in a Presbyterian adult Sunday school class. As part of my address I shared the above illustration; then, I spoke rather forcefully against devoting worship time to a celebration of secular events. After class I went into the morning service and discovered to my chagrin that it was, of all days, Boy Scouts' Day. A number of boy scouts worshiping that Sunday were dressed in their uniforms, as were their leaders. And during worship more than fifteen minutes were devoted to a presentation describing the work of boy scouts and an awards ceremony.

The very next Sunday I was talking to an adult study group in another denomination. Because I had spoken here many times and knew these folks, I felt free to speak my mind. So, in the context of my talk on worship, I told them the boy scout story from the week before. However, before I finished, I noticed a dozen or so people waving their bulletins for me to see. Finally, one person interrupted me and urged, "Look, look at the bulletin." I walked over to the nearest bulletin, looked inside, and discovered to my horror that it was Girl Scout Sunday and that, sure enough, this church was celebrating the Girl Scouts of America! Everyone laughed. But beneath that laughter there was a new sense of awareness, perhaps even an alarm had been set off.

I certainly have nothing against mothers, boy scouts, girl scouts, or Memorial Day. I don't even object to special celebrations of these events by the Christian community, but I do question the propriety of using a morning worship service for such purposes. Morning worship is a time to celebrate the event of Christ's living, dying, and rising for our salvation. I believe we need to refocus on our Christian heritage and the variety of events in Christ's life and, in so doing, restore a sacred sense of time to our worship.

What do I mean by *a sacred sense of time?* Well, the origin of a sacred view of time is found in the Jewish background to the Christian faith. The Hebrews perceived two kinds of time—*kairos* and *chronos. Chronos* is ordinary, moment-to-moment (secular) time. But *kairos* is time that marks a crisis or a turning point in history.

For the Jews, the Exodus was a kairos event because it marked the moment God decisively entered into their history, brought them up out of the land of Egypt, chose them as his people, and entered into a corporate covenant relationship with them.

In Israel, *chronos* was given meaning by the *kairos* events. Festivals which celebrated and relived historically critical moments had the effect of lifting ordinary time into redemptive time. Thus, God's people lived by a sacred year which was rooted in what God had done for them. To celebrate a festival meant much more than just having a good time. It was a way of continually connecting day-to-day life in the world with God's redeeming and saving acts. Feasts were celebrations of the God who was *for Israel*. They were God's feasts by which his saving action for Israel was constantly present.

The Christian approach to time is similar to that of God's people in the Old Testament. Like the Hebrews, Christians also have a *kairos* moment which informs and gives meaning to historical sequence. It is the Christ-event—the birth, life, death, resurrection, ascension, and promised return of the Savior. As Christians, we confess that all time has a center. And that center is Jesus Christ himself who has redeemed all things (see Col. 1:15–23). From this center, this *kairos* event in history, the meaning and significance of all time radiates. It is through the remembrance of the Christ-event in worship that we are able to sanctify all time.

Therefore, time in worship now becomes a means through which we can enter into the service of the King. The church, by recapitulating the *kairos* event, can mystically and symbolically represent time as redeemed and proclaim the birth, life, death, resurrection, coming of the Holy Spirit, and return of Christ. And the worshiping community can reexperience the true meaning of these events and be lifted up in time through its understanding of the Christ-event. In other words, worship is not meant to celebrate Boy Scouts' Day or Mother's Day. Instead it is meant to celebrate the coming of Christ (Advent); the birth of Christ (Christmas); the manifestation of Christ as the light of the whole world (Epiphany); the impending death of Christ (Lent); the events of his last week (Holy Week); the resurrection (Easter); and the coming of the Holy Spirit (Pentecost). These are the kairos events for Christians that give meaning and significance to our day-to-day lives in the world.

I am convinced that we need to restore the sacred sense of time and return to the church year in our worship. And I'd like to suggest two ways in which refocusing our attention on the church year will assist our worship.

THE CHURCH YEAR AS SPIRITUAL PILGRIMAGE

Since the time of the sixteenth-century Reformation, many Protestants have reacted against using the church year calendar as a pattern for worship. "It's a mere formalization of religion"; "It's nothing more than a system of works." Of course there is some truth to these allegations. Any pattern of worship can easily become so formalized that it is nothing more than a sterile, meaningless system.

However, the original intent of worshiping within the framework of the church calendar was to guide the believer in his or her spiritual pilgrimage. Its purpose is to relive the life of Christ, to walk in the footsteps of Jesus, to experience what Jesus experienced, to identify with his earthly life, and through that experience, to grow spiritually.

I recall a conversation with my colleague Joel Sheesley that put the notion of using the church year as a spiritual pilgrimage into perspective for me. We were talking about our journeys in faith when Joel said something like this: "You know, Bob, Christianity was much easier for me when I saw it only as a belief system. I thought everything was all right between God and me because I believed in the Trinity, in the authority of the Bible, in the deity of Christ, in the resurrection and second coming. And when I occasionally detoured in my personal walk with the Lord, it didn't bother me too much. I could always justify my actions by assuring myself that I *believed* in all the right things. But since I've adopted the church year as a guide for my spiritual pilgrimage, my faith seems much more demanding. Faith is no longer a mere system of thought. It is a way of life, a journey into Jesus' life on a day-to-day, moment-by-moment basis. Now when I become lax in my spiritual journey, it's no longer satisfying enough for me to say, 'Well, at least I believe the right things.' I actually hurt on the inside and feel the pain of being out of harmony with Christ."

I've never forgotten this conversation because Joel put his finger on something that I have always struggled with. It's what I call an intellectual Christianity, a Christianity based on understanding. As one who studies and teaches theology for a living, I feel the special danger of making my faith too cerebral. It's easy for all of us to believe the right things and to be orthodox in doctrine, yet unintentionally miss the deep spiritual experience of our faith.

For example, I've never been satisfied with the assumption that I can balance out my intellectualized faith by merely maintaining a daily devotional time. It's not that I'm against this practice. Rather, I struggle with an attitude I've found among many Evangelicals that separates sacred and secular activities. Somewhere in my background I picked up the idea that spirituality consists mainly in setting aside a time for morning and evening devotions. We seem to feel that when we've done that, we've satisfied the Lord. But I've come to believe there is more to my commitment to Christ than that. And for me, that "something more" is in the personal observance of the church year as a spiritual discipline. Let me explain this more fully by walking you through the spiritual disciplines of the seasons of Advent, Christmas, Epiphany, Lent, Holy Week, Easter, and Pentecost.

Advent, that sacred time which begins four Sundays before Christmas, is the season for preparation and anticipation of the coming of Jesus. I think an appropriate analogy to what we do spiritually during Advent is found in what we do physically when a special guest is due to arrive at our home. We "clean house." We wash the windows, vacuum the rugs, scrub the kitchen and bathrooms, polish the furniture, and bake some goodies. In my experience, housecleaning has always been a lot of work and very little fun. Yet, there is an aspect to cleaning house in anticipation of a visit by someone you love that puts all that hard work into another dimension. It's no longer drudgery or a burden when it is done out of a hopeful expectancy. When I clean house because someone special is coming, I always think of the recreation and relaxation that is around the corner.

This motif of preparation and anticipation which is the image of Advent is captured in the personality of John the Baptist. We don't think of John the Baptist as a fun-loving, carefree sport. He comes from the desert wearing a loincloth, eating locusts, and calling on people to repent. His image is sober, solemn, perhaps even severe. Like John the Baptist, we are called during Advent to go into the desert of life and prepare for the coming of Christ. It is a time of renewal, repentance, and self-examination—a time to do some spiritual housecleaning.

I am sure that you, like me, have spent weeks preparing for a visit by loved ones, knowing full well that when they come you will be ready to relax and enjoy their presence. This change in mood from preparing to enjoying is not unlike the shift in spiritual mood from Advent to Christmas.

Simply put, *Christmas* is a season of joy, festivity, and fun. It's a twelve-day festival from December twenty-fifth to January sixth, the day of the Epiphany. And our spiritual experience during this time should be similar to that of enjoying a visit from someone special. It is a time of celebration, of singing Christmas carols, of giving and receiving gifts, of enjoying fellowship with friends and loved ones. This merriment is as much a part of spirituality as are the sober housecleaning days of Advent. During this time we are truly alive and free in the presence of our Guest. And the good news of Jesus Christ deserves a shout, a party, a frolic!

On *Epiphany* the mood shifts once again and our spirituality is pointed in a different direction. On January sixth, we celebrate the visit of the Wise Men. "When they saw the star, they rejoiced exceedingly with great joy; and going into the house they saw the child with Mary his mother, and they fell down and worshiped him" (Matt. 2:10–11). I believe these words capture the essence of Epiphany, the celebration which concludes Christmas and emphasizes that Christ is the Light not only to Israel, but also to the Gentiles and the whole world.

Epiphany, which means "manifestation," is expressed in the New Testament images of the Magi, in the Baptism, and in the early demonstrations of Jesus at the marriage feast in Cana. The central message of each of these events is the manifestation of Jesus as the Christ, the Son of God, the Savior.

The coming of the Magi has been interpreted to mean that the Gospel is to go beyond Israel to the Gentiles. At the Baptism, when the Father's voice identified Jesus as his beloved Son, the secret was out, the Messiah was identified, and his public ministry began. And the turning of water into wine at the marriage feast is a manifestation of the glory and power of Christ.

Epiphany always brings me back to earth, down from the high I've experienced during Christmas. I feel like the party is over and it's back to work, to my own ministry of witness. "How," I ask myself, "am I doing in my calling to manifest Christ? Do people see Christ in me? Am I reflecting the light of Christ? Am I like the salt of the earth?" This is a time for sober reflection on my Christian responsibility. Epiphany challenges me to proclaim Christ, to be bold in my witness for him.

Lent, which begins on Ash Wednesday and continues for forty week days until Easter, represents another shift in the ministry of Jesus and in our spiritual commitment to allow Jesus to take hold of our life through observing the church year as a spiritual discipline. It is definitely the most rigorous and demanding of all the seasons. Nevertheless, I'm always glad I passed through it because of the spiritual challenge it introduces into my life. I come through Lent into Easter feeling that I've passed from death to life once again. My conversion is symbolically repeated and I'm strengthened and encouraged in the faith.

The observance of Lent originated in the early church. It was forty days of intense spiritual discipline for converts who were completing three years of instruction in preparation for an Easter Sunday baptism. Rooted in the history of Moses' forty years in the desert and Christ's forty days in the wilderness, it is meant to be a time of deep spiritual renewal. Gradually, the practice of Lent, which was at first for new converts only, was adopted by the whole church. In this way, baptism and all that it means, both in terms of repentance from sin and renewal to new life, was rehearsed by all.

There was a time when I felt that the observance of Lent was nothing more than a token of Christian discipline. I viewed giving up sweets or some other similarly innocuous thing as a superficial gesture. This practice may be satisfying enough for some, but it is not in keeping with the primary meaning of Lent.

The original idea was to give up a sin that is exercising

power over your life. I find it helpful during Lent to be reminded of the sins that lay claim over my life by reading the baptismal literature of the New Testament. There are a number of lists in the New Testament that give us insight into the disciplines we are to assume if we are truly members of the body of Christ. One of these lists is found in Paul's letter to the Galatian Christians (5:19). Paul lists the sins a person who is converted and baptized into Christ should have no part of. I find an increased awareness of sin in my own life by reading this list at the beginning of Lent. There is always something in my life to work on.

In terms of our spiritual pilgrimage, baptism is the most fitting symbol of Lent. In the New Testament and in the early church baptism signified crossing over from one condition to another. An analogy to baptism is the Exodus; the image of the people of Israel going from their enslavement by Pharaoh across the Red Sea to enter the Promised Land is a picture of baptism. Baptism is a sign of passing from the old state to the new state, from the kingdom of evil to the kingdom of Christ.

I remember my own baptism at age thirteen. My father, the pastor, said, "Robert, do you renounce Satan and all his works?" I said, "I do." And he baptized me in the name of the Father, Son, and Holy Spirit. Lent, which reminds us of our baptism into Christ's death, takes us through that pilgrimage once again. The image is stronger than the housecleaning of Advent because it leads us not to the manger but to the tomb. I like to think of Lent as my opportunity to take my sins into the tomb, to let them die, and to bury them forever. What I do during Lent is what I did when I stood in the baptismal water. I say once again, "I renounce you Satan and all your works."

Of all the baptismal liturgies available, the one in the *Book of Common Prayer* seems to me to summarize best the spirit of my Lenten commitment to put away sin and follow after Christ. Let me share parts of that liturgy with you. Here are a series of questions asked of the candidates for baptism—questions which during Lent each Christian is to commit to once again.

Question: Do you renounce Satan and all the spiritual forces of wickedness that rebel against God?
Answer: I do.
Question: Do you renounce the evil powers of this world which corrupt and destroy the creatures of God?
Answer: I do.
Question: Do you renounce all sinful desires that draw you from the love of God?
Answer: I do.
Question: Do you turn to Jesus and accept him as your Savior?
Answer: I do.
Question: Do you put your whole trust in his grace and love?
Answer: I do.
Question: Do you promise to follow and obey him as your Lord?
Answer: I do.

I was brought up to believe that my conversion experience was a one time act, something I did in the past, something not to be done again. Although I don't believe a person is converted again and again, I do believe that our relationship with God, like a relationship with a spouse, needs to undergo continual renewal and a deepening of commitment. I have found that the experience of Lent leads me into a renewal of my spiritual relationship with Jesus Christ. It is a special forty-day season set aside each year in which I reevaluate my commitment. It is a time when I ask myself, "Am I slipping back into the old ways? Is the devil making some inroads into my life? How has Satan deceived me once again?" During

Lent, I review my baptismal contract with Christ, turn my back on the power and influence of evil, and yield my whole self to Christ as Lord of my life. I've come to the conclusion that I need that intense period of repentance and renewal yearly as an integral part of my spiritual journey.

I can remember how flat my spiritual experience was at Easter when I did not observe Lent. I couldn't feel the resurrection because I had not entered into the death. Now at Easter I can feel the resurrection in my own experience. I'm ready to leave the tomb, roll away the stone, and be raised to new life with Christ. My Lenten experience of symbolically entering the tomb has prepared me to experience the joy and power of the resurrection in a new way.

Perhaps the most significant Easter sermon I've heard recently was a simple statement by the minister. He held out his hands in an upward gesture of openness toward the congregation and with a spirit of joy ringing in his words he said, "What can I say, he is risen from the dead. Christ is risen!" And the whole congregation cried, "He is risen indeed." Then the minister, overwhelmed with the power of the resurrection, shouted, "Alleluia, he is risen from the dead; let us worship him." That was the extent of the sermon and the congregation broke forth in resurrection worship. I was lifted up into the heavens as together we praised God in the heavenly language of "Alleluia, Alleluia, Alleluia!"

The *Easter* season is fifty days of sheer celebration. It is literally a time to celebrate with God's people, to enjoy creation, to revel in relationships, to affirm the great mystery of life, to rejoice in our new life in Christ and in the church, his body. I love the Easter season, especially as it is coupled with spring in the Midwest where I live. The smell of freshly cut grass, the budding of the trees, the shoots of flowers coming up from the moist, thawing ground, the warm rays of the spring sun, the gentle warm breezes, and the cleansing rains are all expressions of the resurrection. The long, cold winter of Lent is gone; the fresh spring of resurrection has me in its grip.

The Easter season ends with *Pentecost,* a celebration of the inrushing presence and power of the Holy Spirit which ushers me into a new experience in my spiritual pilgrimage. We now enter the longest season of the church year which takes us from May through November to the beginning of Advent again.

This time, now called the *Trinity season,* corresponds to the rise and spread of the early church. Christ has ascended into the heavens and commissioned his apostles to be witnesses to the utmost part of the world. My spiritual experience, which from Advent to Pentecost concentrated on following the footsteps of Jesus, turns now to walk the missionary route of the apostles. I travel with Paul to Galatia, Thessalonica, Philippi, Corinth, and Rome. I live with him in jail and travel with him to his last days. This is a time for study, for growth in my interpretation of Christ, for increased depth in my understanding and experience of the church, and for a heightened sensitivity to my social responsibility to the world.

As I now reflect on this brief excursion into the church year as a spiritual pilgrimage and on my own experience over the past few years, I feel a sense of gratitude to the Holy Spirit who has gifted God's people with this pattern for living out the life of Christ. But I am also reminded that there is another dimension to it, namely the varied Christian experience it gives to God's people. And without this experience, it seems to me we miss something of the great glory and richness of our Christian faith.

THE CHURCH YEAR AS A PATTERN FOR CORPORATE WORSHIP

Over the course of the past few years I have made it a special point to ask pastors of evangelical churches what they would like to see happen in the worship of their congregations. Frequently, the response to this question is a desire to return to following the church year as a pattern for worship. In particular, their interest has focused on worship during Advent and the Holy Week. This shift seems to be motivated by a growing need for a corporate spiritual experience.

Many renewed churches are moving away from an individualistic concept of the church in which worship is perceived as private, personal, and subjective. Individualism is being replaced by the realization that the church is the *people* among whom the mystery of God in Christ reconciling the world to himself is experienced. And part of this shift toward a community experience is the participation of the local church in the universal Christian practice of following the journey of our Lord's work on earth through the sacred year. It means something to me, for example, to know that my worship on a particular Sunday, such as the first Sunday in Advent, is the same experience of anticipating Christ's coming that is celebrated by Christians in Poland and Africa.

Yet, I can understand why Protestants in general moved away from patterning their worship after the church year. By the late medieval era, the church was becoming so overcrowded with saints' days and festivals that the actual rhythm of Christ's birth, life, death, and resurrection was often hidden from view. The events of Christ which the church year intends to reenact had actually become lost in the maze of secondary feasts and celebrations.

In this context, the Reformer, John Calvin, understandably swung to the other side of the pendulum. He dropped the entire church year, the good with the bad. He developed a defense against the church calendar, arguing that it was an invention of the Roman church, that it was a discipline of "works" not of faith, and that since its observance was not explicitly taught in the Bible, it should not be followed.

After the sixteenth century, almost all Protestants

joined Calvin in his rejection of the church year. For example, in the seventeenth century the Puritans influenced Parliament to order December twenty-fifth to be maintained as a fast day. Troops were even ordered to check houses in London to see that no Christmas dinners were being cooked. And this rejection of Christmas and other Christian feast days was brought to America through the influence of the Pilgrim fathers and the Puritans.

But today we face another problem. By not following the Christian calendar we have come to adopt secular guidelines for our spiritual time. Christ has again become lost in our celebration of time, not because of too many saints' days and feasts, but because of our celebration in worship of too many other days—national holidays like Independence Day and special events like Mother's Day.

It is important to our thinking that we ask ourselves this: What does our worship represent? If we can agree that worship does represent Christ, his birth, life, death, and resurrection, then it is imperative for our spiritual health to restore the rhythm of Christ to our worship services. As the community of God's people we can do this by celebrating the life and work of our Lord not only in our weekly services, but in the yearly cycle of our worship. It seems to me this is already happening in many of our churches. We are beginning to return to the observance of a simple church year—one which emphasizes Christ without the interference of those complex feasts and saints' days that once hid the real meaning of the church year from view.

I believe the current move toward following the cycle of the church year will assist us in recovering the variety in worship which so many evangelicals feel is a priority. I have found that worship which does not follow the church year is often characterized by sameness. Sermons are built around the study of a particular biblical book or a series on the Lord's prayer, the Beatitudes, the Ten

Commandments, and the fruits of the spirit. This pattern is then interrupted only by the "special" Sundays of Christmas, Easter, Mother's Day, and so on. For me, this has become a routine that tends to dull the richness of our faith. But worse than that is the experience of having major feast days such as Christmas and Easter go by without adequate preparation for them and no larger context in which they can be understood. This is a trend of secularism that an increasing number of Christian people want to avoid.

The church calendar year provides us not only with a variety of events to celebrate, but also with varied periods of intensity and relaxation in our worship. This rhythm fits my own nature because I can function no better at a pitched intensity without relief than I can at a continuously slow pace of sameness.

The Christian observance of time is divided between extraordinary time and ordinary time (not to be confused with secular). Extraordinary time refers to those *kairos* events in which God revealed himself, through which he redeemed the world, and by which he calls a people to himself. They are the major events such as Christmas and Easter which reenact the birth and resurrection of our Lord. They constitute the memory of the church. Consequently, they are the times we are chiefly to celebrate.

Extraordinary time within the church is divided into two cycles. The first cycle is the cycle of light which includes Advent, Christmas, and Epiphany and proclaims Christ as the Light of the world. It begins with the lighting of Advent candles which remind us that the Light of the world is soon to be born. Epiphany emphasizes the spread of Light to the whole world and brings the cycle of light to an end. Through the cycle of light we not only celebrate the birth of Christ as the Light of the world on Christmas Day, but continue to celebrate it for seven weeks (approximately) at the beginning of every Christian year.

The second cycle is the cycle of life which begins with Lent. It is the time during which we enter into preparation for the death of Christ. We are taken into the rejection of Christ, even into his tomb, and brought through the resurrection, the highest point of Christian celebration. During this time we celebrate our new life in Christ. The cycle of life ends with Pentecost and the coming of the Holy Spirit.

Ordinary time differs from extraordinary time in that it is not characterized by a central significant event which the church celebrates. Its meaning and importance are derived instead from the events of extraordinary time. Ordinary time is not less important. Rather, it's a breather from the intensity of extraordinary time. It's a time during which the meaning of extraordinary time may have its effect and may be applied to everyday life.

My most unforgettable experience of being lifted out of ordinary time into the extraordinary occurred at a time when I was just beginning to be sensitized to the need for worship renewal in my own life. Easter was near and I wanted to experience the resurrection of Christ in a new, vital way. So a friend of mine suggested I attend the Easter eve paschal vigil, a service dating back to the ancient church, which would be celebrated in many local liturgical churches. I chose to participate in the service of St. Michael's Catholic Church, near my home in Wheaton.

I did not know anyone in the church, nor had I heard much about the congregation, although I had heard from a reliable source that the church's young, energetic, charismatic assistant priest had turned a number of people on to the Scriptures and a renewed sense of worship. That was good enough for me. I wanted to go. I wanted to celebrate the resurrection of Christ in a different way. But as I entered the parking lot, I wondered what I was getting myself into. Little did I know.

I was somewhat apprehensive as I walked up to the huge wooden door and grasped its brass handle. But I took a deep breath and pulled. To my astonishment I had entered a huge vestibule that was absolutely pitch dark inside. As I stepped inside, I bumped into another body and sensed immediately that the vestibule was full of people. No one was talking, not even a whisper. Not knowing what to do or what was going to be done, I simply stood in my spot now squeezed on all sides by several other bodies. My imagination began to soar as I felt myself in the tomb with Christ, and a quivering sensation penetrated my body as I stood there in quiet expectancy.

Suddenly, without warning, a huge light flared up in the vestibule and the young priest sang out, "The light of Christ," in a clear, resonant voice that literally rang in the vestibule and echoed off the walls. And the congregation responded by singing, "Thanks be to God." My whole body felt as though it had been penetrated by that light and the sound of the refrain. My spirit leaped within me in response, and I felt the awesome presence of the Holy Spirit moving in that vestibule almost as if the stone of the tomb were being rolled away. The priest, his attendants, the acolytes, and an assembled choir began moving toward the center door leading into the sanctuary.

Soon, we were all in a huge procession following the priest who held in both hands a four-foot-long, white paschal candle. Just as I thought of Christ, the Light of the world, moving from the tomb, the procession came to a halt. Not knowing what to do I simply kept my eyes on the priest. In time, he slowly lifted the huge candle high above his head and once again loudly and forcefully sang those words that were breaking the long, arduous Lent and paving the way for the resurrection, "The light of Christ." For a third time we moved down the center aisle and stopped to see the candle lifted high and to hear those glorious words, "The light of Christ." As we responded, "Thanks be to God," I felt myself overcome with a new sense of the importance of the event we were

celebrating, and my eyes filled with tears of joy and gratitude.

We continued to stand as the priest set the paschal
candle in a central place near the Table of the Lord and
sang the *Exsultet.* Here was a priest who was not doing
something rote and mechanical. He felt what he was singing and that feeling was communicated to me as I stood
drinking in the message of the night. I can still recall
the chill that ran through my whole being as I listened
to the priest sing:

> This is the night, when all who believe in Christ are delivered
> from the gloom of sin, and are restored to grace and holiness
> of life.
>
> This is the night, when Christ broke the bonds of death and
> hell, and rose victorious from the grave.
>
> IIow blessed is this night, when earth and heaven are joined
> and man is reconciled to God.

These and other refrains were sung in the church now
lit *only* by the light of the single paschal candle. I glanced
around me at the dim, flickering light on the faces of
God's people who had come there to celebrate this awesome event. I felt as though I was participating in the
original event when Satan was sent into flight and God's
Son rose victorious as the light that dispels all darkness.

The service continued for two more hours with Scripture readings, a baptism, and a glorious Eucharist celebrating the resurrection of Jesus from the dead. It was the
most significant Easter of my life. I had been lifted out
of the ordinary and mundane and brought into the extraordinary event of Christ's resurrection from the dead.
It was a taste of new wine, and the beginning of a new
pursuit—the search for an experience of Christ in worship.

The road I have taken is filled with people who, like myself, feel the need for "something more" in worship. And what we are experiencing in the recovery of the church year is not something new or gimmicky. The church year is a gift to the church given by the Holy Spirit as a way of enriching our relationship to Jesus Christ—of restoring a sacred sense of time to our worship. It has withstood the test of time and demonstrated by its staying power that it is worthy of our adoption today.

CHAPTER NINE

Rediscover the Arts

Previously in this book I described my experience of worshiping in both a Russian Orthodox Church and a Plymouth Brethren Church. In each case I walked away from the service feeling satisfied, as though I had truly worshiped. Yet, the contrast in the physical setting of these churches is as great as that between day and night.

I shall never forget the dazzling beauty of the Church of the Holy Trinity in downtown Moscow. When I opened the door of that church, I felt as though I was stepping out of earth into heaven itself, as though I was experiencing a heavenly vision like the one St. John described in Revelation 4 and 5:

A throne stood in heaven, with one seated on the throne! And he who sat there appeared like jasper and carnelian, and round the throne was a rainbow that looked like an emerald. Round the throne were twenty-four thrones, and seated on the thrones were twenty-four elders, clad in white garments, with golden crowns upon their heads. From the throne issue flashes of lightning, and voices and peals of thunder, and before the throne burn seven torches of fire, which are the seven spirits of God; and before the throne there is as it were a sea of glass, like crystal (4:2–6).

As I walked through the doors of that great cathedral and entered inside, I saw people—hundreds and hundreds of them standing shoulder-to-shoulder in every nook and cranny of that great church. And the magnificent splendor which surrounded these people created an awe-inspiring atmosphere. Everywhere I turned I sensed the presence of Christ, the apostles, the prophets, and saints in iconographic description.

The Orthodox believe that in worship the congregation actually experiences a foretaste of the second coming of Christ in glory and comes into the presence of the entire heavenly congregation. That is, heaven and earth, the future and the present, meet in worship.

Here I was, standing at the back of the church, in the midst of all this beauty. My eyes drifted upward, and I noticed the great fresco of the triumphant Christ in the center dome. Christ—the Lord of the universe, the Teacher and Preacher of the Gospel, the Judge of the world—watched, as it were, over all. My heart skipped a beat as I felt myself pulled up into his very presence, joining the tens of thousands of choirs and the cherubim and seraphim in the great antiphonal chorus, "Holy, Holy, Holy, is the Lord Almighty. The whole earth is full of his glory."

My eyes then dropped from the center dome to the front of the sanctuary, where the iconostasis, a screen holding paintings of the heavenly personalities, was located. There I saw icons of Christ, of his mother, Mary, and of his predecessor, John the Baptist. On the royal doors leading behind the screen to the altar were icons of the archangels Gabriel and Michael. Above them all, in a second row, were depictions of the apostles; in a third row, the saints and martyrs of the Church; and in a final fourth row, the prophets of the Old Testament. My heart quickened as I sensed that I was home with my family, worshiping with my brothers and sisters in the faith, the whole company of God's people, the communion of the saints.

I was moved by the biblical scenes painted on the wall. Here was Jesus at his dedication by Simeon. There he was talking to the Pharisees and Sadducees at the Temple. I saw him turning water into wine, raising Lazarus from the dead, and healing the sick. And the fire of candles, which cast their lengthened shadows across the pictures of Jesus and the heavenly host, surrounded it all.

In a rare moment of spiritual release, the aesthetic side of my person was set free to worship God. Color, sound, light, texture, and smell lifted me up into the praise of God, and I felt as though I was joining all creation in the praise of his blessed and holy name.

My experience in the Plymouth Brethren Church was quite different. As I entered the narthex of the Brethren Church, I noticed people were talking in hushed whispers and moving quickly to their seats. I stood momentarily at the entrance to the sanctuary and quickly glanced around me. It was, of course, a very simple setting. The church sanctuary was square, with white walls and tall clear windows on both sides. At the face of the church, a raised chancel accommodated a pulpit in the center and a plain table in the front on which the words "This Do in Remembrance of Me" were inscribed. Three chairs sat behind the pulpit and to the left a piano.

Although the sanctuary was simple and unadorned, an air of quiet expectancy breathed among the people. They sat with heads bowed in a posture of prayer. Some were reading Scriptures, others were meditating on a hymn. But no one was talking or moving around. There was a stillness, a sense of preparation in those people that I could feel within myself. I quietly tiptoed to my seat and joined them in prayer as we together began to meet the Lord in the hush of his presence.

The sense that *all* creation joins in worship was as present in this church as it was in the Russian Orthodox Church. Indeed, color, light, sound, and smell were not as obviously incorporated into the service, but the pulpit, the Communion Table, and the bread and wine were visible symbols that expressed the congregation's thanks-giving. And I was able to join that group of God's people and turn my heart to sing him praises.

These two illustrations point to the extreme ends of a debate that has divided Christians throughout the centuries—just how much and to what extent the use of art forms is permissible in worship.

The Orthodox position is founded in the Old Testament. These worshipers point to the elaborate artistic beauty of the tabernacle and the temple. If God permitted our senses to be involved in worship in the Old Testament, they ask, why would he forbid it in the New Testament? They also cite the example of the incarnation. Look, they say, God became a man—a human, visible, material, sensual person. If God can communicate himself to us through a created body, why can't we respond similarly to him through color, sound, movement, smell, touch, and sight?

On the other side of the issue, Protestants draw their position from the second commandment: "You shall not make for yourself a graven image, or any likeness of anything that is in heaven above, or that is in the earth beneath, or that is in the water under the earth; you shall not bow down to them or serve them; for I the Lord your God am a jealous God" (Exod. 20:4). They interpret these words as a command against the use of any icons, frescos, or statues that depict heavenly images. Yet, many Protestants acknowledge that this verse does not specifically deny or forbid the use of such items as candles, incense, vestments, processions, musical instruments, choirs, stained glass windows, door and furniture carvings, artistically designed pulpits, tables, or baptismal fonts.

So why, then, do we Protestants have such plain settings for our worship? The issue boils down to a difference of opinion articulated during the sixteenth-century Reformation by John Calvin on the one hand and Martin Luther and the Anglicans on the other. Luther and the Anglicans believed that *whatever is not explicitly rejected by the Scripture may be used in worship.* Consequently, they were free to use the ceremonial quite liberally. But Calvin believed *only that which is explicitly taught in the New Testament is permissible in worship.* Since the New Testament says nothing pro or con about the use of art in worship, Calvinists and their successors were not free to employ the arts as means of expressing worship to Almighty God.

We cannot hope to solve an age-old controversy here. So, let it be sufficient for me to ask the Protestant community for a second consideration of some of the least controversial issues related to using the arts in worship. I want to suggest that we increase our use of the arts such as music, drama, dance, space, and color.

I do not want to be misunderstood. I'm not arguing that art is *necessary* for worship. Certainly we can worship God anywhere and under any conditions. To insist that art is necessary for worship is to commit aesthetic heresy. Such insistence makes art an idol, an object of our worship. On the other hand, to insist that art is a hinderance to worship is equally dangerous. It denies that the material creation is a worthy vehicle through which God can communicate to us, and we to him. Ultimately it denies the incarnation, for it was in human, material flesh that God became present to us in Jesus Christ. Assuming then that we desire to avoid such extremes, we may ask the question: What is the function of art in worship? Let me answer that by telling you about a recent birthday celebration in our home.

Because birthdays are important occasions, most of us like to celebrate them in ways that express their importance. In my family, we like to think of certain birthdays as turning points. We look at thirteen, sixteen, and twenty-one as decisive events for our children. Thirteen represents the move into teens; sixteen signifies a new degree of freedom with license to drive and permission to date; and twenty-one represents maturity and leaving the nest. For adults, thirty, forty, fifty, and sixty-five seem to be the magic numbers.

On the occasion of my fiftieth, my wife wanted to do something special for me. After much consideration, she decided to have a small dinner party for the family and a few of our closest friends. I watched (and helped) for more than two days as she worked to prepare the house, the meal, and the table for this festive celebration.

On the night before the party, everything was finished except those things that can be done only at the last minute. Every room in the house had been thoroughly cleaned. The furniture was polished, the windows were shining, and everything was in its proper place. But the dining room had received the most attention. A beautiful new tablecloth draped the table which was decorated with a special arrangement of flowers, new candles, and the finest of our china, silverware, and goblets.

My wife had also selected carefully some of my favorite foods for this birthday feast. The appetizers included shrimp, marinated mushrooms, hot artichokes, clam dip, and cheese spinach balls. The main course consisted of honey-baked ham, scalloped potatoes, broccoli smothered in cheese sauce, tossed spinach salad, and a sweet potato soufflé. And the dessert, of course, was a cake with fifty candles and my favorite ice cream.

It was a wonderful and special occasion for me. Sure, we could have saved ourselves the trouble and gone out to a nice restaurant for an elegantly prepared meal. But somehow, although that would have represented food and company, it wouldn't have been the same. What made my birthday so special was the fact that the house, the table, and the meal became symbols of love and celebration. Because they actually embodied the meaning of the celebration, they acted as aids and assists to the celebration. They made the birthday party joyous and festive.

The function of art in worship is similar to the role of the clean house, the beautifully decorated dining room, and the lovingly prepared meal in a birthday celebration. It embodies the occasion in such a way that the event is served. Just as the house, the table, and the food turned my birthday into a special occasion, so art forms turn worship into a special event, serving it, assisting it, creating it.

In this chapter, I want to extend and apply the fourth principle of worship—*all creation joins in worship*—by illustrating how various arts can serve worship and make it more joyous and festive.

Music

My friend Mary Hopper, a music professor at Wheaton College tells me that the purpose of music is to serve the message. "We bring music to the sacred text," she says. "Music lifts up the theme; it puts it into another setting, and expresses it." Recently, I attended an All Saints' Day worship service in which the principle that music serves the text seemed to be abundantly clear.

On the days previous to the service, we had helped our younger children create costumes to don for their door-to-door journey in search of treats on Halloween, the commercialized and secular version of All Saints' Day. Of course, we had our bowl of candy bars and bubble gum ready at the door to give out to all the other neighborhood kids. Our preparations for Halloween had been made within the context of television and newspaper advertisements urging us to see the latest ghost movies and horror stories. So, it was with a sense of relief that I went to an All Saints' Day worship. Here the music served the biblical text of Revelation 5, the depiction of all the saints in heaven worshiping. I put thoughts of a commercial Halloween behind me and my spirits were lifted high as I experienced my oneness with all the saints of God. The organ music swelled into full volume and the congregation sang with great conviction: "For all the saints, who from their labors rest, for thee by faith before the world confessed, thy Name, O Jesus, be forever blest. Alleluia, alleluia!" Heaven seemed to open up, and there I was, with my loved ones and friends who have gone on to glory, standing as it were around the throne, worshiping and praising God.

Protestants don't need to be told about the value of music in worship. A great contribution of Protestantism to worship is its hymnody. But perhaps we need to be reminded how music serves the order of worship and the seasons of the year.

First, I believe music serves the fourfold order of Preparation, hearing the Word, communing at the Table, and being sent forth. Through its lyrics, melody, and rhythm, music brings us into the presence of God, assists us in hearing and responding to the Word, helps us experience healing at the Communion Table, and provides us with the sense of being sent forth. Because this seems so simple I am always astonished when I worship in a church that doesn't seem to have this sense. To sing, for example, a hymn such as "O Worship the King, All Glorious Above" at the Dismissal is out of order, because it is a hymn that serves the preparation of our hearts to worship and typically belongs in the first part of the service. It represents the beginning of a public worship service, not the end. In a situation where music is at odds with what is supposed to be happening, my whole sense of order and sequence in my approach to God is thrown out of kilter. My worship is distorted and disjointed, and my spirit becomes confused and misplaced. I find such a situation so distracting that my stomach becomes tense and I'm no longer free to worship.

The same principle is applicable to the seasons of the church year. Since the texts of the lectionary readings take us through the church year, music selections which do not serve the text distract, confuse, and run counter to the spiritual pilgrimage we are following during a particular season.

For example, I find music during the cycle of light to be highly joyful. During Advent I love to sing the hymn "Come Thou Long Expected Jesus," because it creates within me a feeling of anticipation for the birth of Christ. Similarly, during Christmas I catch myself constantly singing carols because they express a sense of fulfillment that Christ has come and the world is full of joy and hope. During Epiphany I enjoy singing "We Three Kings of Orient Are" because this hymn expresses the discovery of Christ by the Gentile world of which I am a part. In this way, music during the cycle of light assists me in the spiritual experience of anticipating Christ, of rejoicing in his birth, and of sensing that he is indeed the light that goes beyond Israel to include the whole world.

As the church year shifts from the cycle of light into the cycle of life, the mood of my spiritual experience also changes. I again find that music assists my spiritual journey through Lent. Because Lent is a penitential season in which identification with Christ's suffering and death intensifies, the music of that season takes on a sober, repentant, and introspective mood. I sing the words "with broken heart and contrite sigh, a trembling sinner, Lord, I cry: Thy pardoning grace is rich and free: O God, be merciful to me." How spiritually awkward it would be, for example, to sing during Lent, "Welcome, happy morning! Age to Age shall say: Hell today is vanquished, heaven is won today," the words from an Easter hymn. However, in order to really *feel* the power of "Welcome, happy morning," I need to sing "with broken heart" during Lent. Spiritually, I need music that takes me into the tomb before I can enjoy the music that rolls away the stone and helps me shout, "Alleluia!"

The somber music of Lent helps me prepare for Easter by creating within me a feeling of solemnity. In my church we don't even use the organ during Holy Week.

We go back to the Gregorian tones that work well without accompaniment. Because celebrative music has been taken away from me and replaced by a music that expresses the solemn spirit of Holy Week, I feel more prepared to truly celebrate the joy of the resurrection.

Easter, of course, is the highest and most joyful season of the Christian year. It's the time to pull out all the stops and let the music ring. Unlike that of any other season, Easter music contains a mystical element which has a way of bringing me through the experience of the death and the resurrection of Christ. In my church we don't sing any "Alleluias" during Lent, but on Easter Sunday the service rejoices with "Alleluias." The singing of the "Alleluias" together with the rest of the joyful music of Easter floods my heart and soul with tremendous praise and happiness. The experience of feeling the resurrection as an event occurring in my own life surpasses the quality of simply remembering an event that happened two thousand years ago. It becomes a vital experience, a present reality which I feel and live now. And music plays a major role in that experience because it uplifts me and unleashes a response within me which is untapped by mere words.

I find that both on a weekly and a yearly basis music helps and assists my worship. It puts my offering of praise and thanksgiving into an ordered setting. It keeps my worship from becoming haphazard or chaotic. It provides direction and meaning to my spiritual life because it is patterned after the life of Christ as expressed throughout the church year. So, while music is an offering to God, it also has the effect of spiritual formation in my own life. It directs my experience in Christ and aids me in personal identification with the birth, suffering, death, and resurrection of Christ.

Art

My friend Alva Steffler, professor of art at Wheaton College, calls art a "visual voice." When art speaks in worship, "it brings order out of chaos," he says. For Steffler, the orderliness of art "speaks to me about God, who he is, and how we relate to him as creatures." This is because our own spiritual life is "an ordering out of chaos, a definition due to design." For that reason, says Steffler, good art "speaks to me. It makes me listen. It forms me."

Although historically Protestants are not known for their use of art in worship, the function of art needs to be addressed because of an increased interest in the use of banners, multimedia, and other visual objects of art. The growing practice of incorporating art in worship is intended to assist and expand congregational sensitivity to the various seasons of the church year.

Let me take you back to the Advent service we celebrated at Wheaton College (described in chapter 1). For this service, Alva Steffler prepared a single banner which hung at the front of the college chapel. He purchased a thirty-foot-long and six-foot-wide red velvet cloth on which he printed in large, bold white letters the biblical passage "Prepare ye the way of the Lord." Since the chapel ceiling is more than fifty feet high and the chapel is greater than one hundred feet wide, the banner was not overwhelming, rather, it aesthetically filled the space.

This highly visible bright banner was a powerful reminder to me of the theme of Advent, the theme of Christ's coming. In my own private devotion and in public worship when I sang, heard the Scripture, and took Communion, my imagination continually re-created that vision of the banner with its message to prepare for the coming of Christ. It was a constant message, a mental picture that ordered and directed my spiritual pilgrimage during Advent.

However, in choosing to use art we must be careful not to distract or inhibit the spirit of the worshiping community with art that is poorly done.

Another striking example of the use of art in worship may be illustrated from a service that Mary Hopper, Joel

Sheesley, and I led during Lent in the Wheaton College Chapel. There is an ancient spiritual tradition which was developed in the fourth century that is designed to follow the footsteps of Jesus from his condemnation to his burial. This tradition, used mainly in the Catholic Church, has come to be known as the "stations of the cross." Most Catholic churches have artistic depictions of the fourteen stations or moments in the life of Jesus located on the walls of the sanctuary. On Fridays during Lent, Catholics will gather to hear Scripture and prayers read at each of these stations. More recently this service is being adopted by Protestants.

Joel Sheesley, who has an outstanding ability to create modern religious art, painted modern depictions of these fourteen stations on canvas, then photographed them and turned them into slides for our chapel. Since it is impossible for a congregation of over two thousand people to move from station to station, we chose three students to symbolize the congregation's journey from one station to another as the slides were flashed on the screen in a semi-darkened room. These students were dressed in black gowns. One of them carried a large wooden cross and the other two acted as attendants and moved down the center aisle as each leg of the journey was portrayed on the screen.

At each station I announced the theme of the depiction (i.e., Jesus is condemned to death), read the appropriate Scripture, and led in prayer. Then the congregation sang one verse of a hymn. After a short period of silence, we proceeded to the next theme. As we moved closer to the end, the three moving participants demonstrated with their body gestures the meaning of the station. At station ten—Jesus is stripped of his garments—they quietly knelt; at station eleven—Jesus is nailed to the cross—they lifted their arms stretching them painfully toward the figure of the suffering Christ; at station twelve—Jesus dies on the cross—they laid prostrate on the floor, their bodies outstretched in the form of total penitence. Their lifeless forms remained in this motionless position as we acted out stations thirteen and fourteen—the body of Jesus is placed in the arms of his mother and Jesus is laid in the tomb. During these last stations we sang the verse "Were you there when they laid him in the tomb?" The singing was soft and tender, without organ accompaniment. Hundreds of us were moved to tears and sang with quivering voice as the art depicting the final suffering of our Lord became a "visual voice." My experience of Holy Week was ordered by that worship event and I longed for Jesus to rise up out of the tomb in victory over the power of death.

These are only a few of many possible examples of the ways in which art can express the message. But I have found that art always impresses me. Somehow the art in worship surrounds me and gathers me up into itself. Like music, it enters into my soul and abides there. During the week it becomes a dominant image in my experience and pulls me into its message. It causes me to dwell on the theme and allows the theme to dwell in me. In this way, it forms me and energizes my spiritual pilgrimage during that season.

Drama

Drama is another art form that is making a slow but certain return to worship. I have already suggested that worship itself is a kind of drama containing a script and players. The content of the drama is the life, death, resurrection, ascension, and return of Christ. The players are the members of the congregation together with the worship leaders who prompt the players as they tell and act out the story of the work of Christ.

David Mains has a special interest in the use of drama in worship. According to him, "The biggest problem with drama in worship is that people try to pack it with content." Drama, he says, "is an art form that draws on the emotions. It is a means of drawing people into the content."

Some churches are using drama as a way of drawing people into the Scripture reading or the sermon. For example, Pastor Ames Broen told me how on one Sunday during the reading of John 21 he had a small group of costumed actors re-create the throwing of the net and eating the breakfast of fish by the Sea of Galilee. On another Sunday, when his sermon had to do with the entrance into Jerusalem, Broen walked down into the congregation and started preaching from the center aisle. He said, "I attempted to give them the feeling that we were walking to Jerusalem together, telling them what we would see as we were coming down the streets."

Pastor Neil Garrabrant told me of an incident he staged when he preached on "barriers of communication between people." During his sermon, two young men came up the center aisle and stood on either side of a partition that had been built especially for the occasion. They briefly shouted objections to each other, but did not communicate because of the barrier between them. Although this drama was less than two minutes in length, it illustrated the sermon's essential message: the importance of breaking down the barriers that exist between people in the church.

I don't think it would be wise to dramatize Scripture or the sermon's message every Sunday. However, I do feel an occasional, nicely executed dramatization makes an unforgettable impression on the worshiper.

In our church, on the first Sunday in Advent, a layman dressed in tattered clothes portrayed John the Baptist calling for repentance and preparation for the coming of Christ. For a moment, I felt transported back into the time of Christ and sensed that I was standing in the presence of John the Baptist. The memory of this portrayal of John still comes to mind every Advent. It calls me now, as it did then, into personal repentance and preparation for the coming of Christ.

My personal experience of drama in the church is that it can be used quite effectively during each season of the church year. For example, my worship in Advent is always enriched by the lighting of the candles which anticipate the birth of Christ. I feel Advent happening when each Sunday a new candle is lit to portray the coming of the Savior. Then on Christmas, when the fifth candle in the center is finally lit, I feel a sense of the completion of Advent and the arrival of Christ in Bethlehem. It's a tradition that signifies that Christ, the Light of the world, has come to dispel not only the darkness of the world, but the darkness that still seeks to make its home inside me.

I'm also moved during Lent by the dramatic effect of the solemn procession at the beginning of the service. Somehow the grave nature of Lent is more effectively communicated to me when the choir members, followed by the pastor and other leaders of worship, march to their places in utter silence. On occasion I have watched the pastor and worship leaders stop at the end of the aisle and lie prostrate on the floor for a short time. This drama is usually done without music in a sanctuary that has been stripped of banners, bright colors, and other signs of life in an effort to create an atmosphere of sobriety. Often a branch without leaves or any sign of life is placed where the flowers usually go. These dramatic portrayals assist my spirit in its pilgrimage into the tomb, into the cycle of death.

One year, as part of Holy Week, Countryside Chapel dramatized the crucifixion. Pastor Neil Garrabrant describes it: "In the front of the church we placed a large wooden cross with spikes on it. All the lights were out except for a spotlight on the cross. We then played the tape entitled 'The Crucifixion.' It's a drama of Christ on

the cross. The narrative is that of the people at the foot
of the cross calling Jesus names, chiding him to come
down from the cross. Part of the drama was the actual
hammering of the nails. It was a powerful presentation
of the cross and of Christ's suffering. We could have ended
the service right there."

The next year the same cross was used on Easter. The
congregation celebrated the service in two parts. The
first dramatized the crucifixion, and the second emphasized the resurrection. According to Garrabrant, "People
feel these symbols help them focus more on the spiritual
meaning of the event . . . it makes it real."

Drama can be, as these illustrations suggest, a powerful
tool for communicating a message in a way that helps
worshipers remember it. Unfortunately, I have also experienced a few situations in which a dramatic presentation
was done so poorly that it interfered with the message.
These occasions make me realize that as we Evangelicals
continue to discover the place of drama in worship.
Whether it is in the reading of Scripture, in illustrating
the sermon, or in fleshing out the drama of the sacred
season, it is important that our drama is appropriate to
the occasion and that it serves the message, not dominates
it.

Dance

Recently I gave a series of lectures on worship at an
evangelical college faculty worship. As I was planning
my talks, I consulted with several faculty members about
the content of my speeches. I asked one of them, "Should
I make some comments about the use of dance in worship?" The immediate response was, "No, I don't think
so. People here are not open to dance." On this person's
recommendation I chose not to mention the role of dance
in worship. However, during the question and answer
period, another faculty member asked, "What do you

think about dance in worship?" I told the faculty why I had chosen not to address that particular subject and was surprised when my comments drew a huge laugh from the audience. As it turned out, the majority of faculty members in this very conservative school were open to liturgical dance. (Liturgical dance must be distinguished from social dancing. It is simply an expressive use of the body similar to that used by David who danced before the Lord.)

Susan Fay, a liturgical dance teacher at Wheaton College, told me that in her classes and workshops she always discusses the rationale for dance in worship. "We really have to rethink this Hellenistic mind-body dichotomy that teaches that the material is evil and the spiritual is good," she says. "After all, God created the whole world and our bodies as well . . . so there can be nothing inherently evil with the body. Also, we are told to love God with our whole heart, mind, and body. I think that includes using our physical bodies in worship."

I asked Mrs. Fay how she justifies dance from a biblical point of view. She said, "I hate to segment the Bible into the Old and New Testament and act as if the Old Testament doesn't count any more." "Dance," she continued, "is certainly a natural part of worship in the Old Testament. It was never censured so I think we can take it as exemplary."

Recently I attended an ordination service in a nearby Baptist church. Prior to the celebration of the Lord's Supper, a teenage girl danced before the Communion Table as the choir sang the *agnus dei* (Lamb of God). As she walked silently in veneration and dignity up the center aisle and stood reverently before the Table that was raised at the back of the chancel area, a sense of the power of communication through the media of movement was already anticipated by the congregation. She was dressed in a long black gown with a bright red sash tied around her waist. In her right hand was a freshly baked, broken loaf of bread and in her left hand she held a silver chalice. Both the bread and the chalice were raised above her head with her arms crossed in the form of an X, one of the many signs of the cross. She laid the bread and the wine on the Table in a gesture of humility and prayer and knelt before the elements.

As the choir sang "Lamb of God," she sprang into action, with her right arm shooting up beyond her outstretched body as though she was reaching up into the heavens. Then suddenly both arms were outstretched upward. The choir continued, "Who takes away the sins of the world," and the dancer's arms swiftly and gracefully moved downward in the action of taking away our sins and putting them away forever. "Have mercy on us," the choir sang strongly as her whole body gracefully knelt, back and shoulders bent down, head slightly raised, and arms dropped to the side as a sign of resignation and repentance.

Again, "Lamb of God who takes away the sins of the world" was sung as the dancer took the bread and wine in her hands and thrust them heavenward as if to remind God of the symbols he himself gave us as signs of his everlasting love and commitment to us through the sacrifice of his Son. Swiftly, the dancer thrust the chalice heavenward, then the bread, back and forth as the choir sang until she stood erect with both arms raised holding the cup and bread high and lifted up for all to see.

As the choir came to a conclusion, singing, "Grant us thy peace," the dancer twirled with the cup and bread held high, at first fast, then slowly. Finally, she faced the congregation as a sign of God hearing the prayer for us. She quietly and peacefully settled her body on the floor, and seated on her crossed legs, she lowered her head, shoulders, and back in a signal of perfect peace and rest. The tension was over and the battle won. Peace was granted at last and a muffled sigh was heard from the congregation who, having been caught up in the petition for mercy, now experienced the grace and peace of the Lamb of God who takes away the sins of the world.

I don't think we need to fear this kind of liturgical dance. It certainly will not turn us into worldly Christians, nor impede our worship or produce unclean thoughts. Rather, spiritual dance will trigger our worship, our praise, and our adoration of the God who saves us in Jesus Christ. It's another way to help us respond to God and his great love.

Space

Frank Lloyd Wright, one of the most famous of the twentieth-century architects, who is known not only for his buildings, but also for the philosophy that motivated his work, once said, "We shape our environment, then our environment shapes us." If this is true for our homes, our schools, our places of business, our parks, and our recreational centers, then isn't it also true for our churches?

It is my experience that the architecture of our church is shaped by our concept of worship, which in turn shapes our experience of worship. Robert Taylor, a church architect from Wheaton, Illinois, refers to his architecture as "a physical envelope in which worship is going to take place." A building together with its furnishing and arrangement of space is a physical expression of a particular congregation's attitude toward worship. Taylor points out that "in a church that places an emphasis on the sacraments, you'll find the focal point to be the altar; in a church that places its principal emphasis on the proclamation of the Word, you'll find the pulpit is usually the most prominent; and in churches where a great deal of emphasis is placed on baptism by immersion, the baptistry is usually a strong focal point."

Throughout this book I have argued for a balance between the Word of God and the Table of our Lord. In worship, both the Bible and the bread and wine are equally important means through which Christ is proclaimed. If this is true, then those congregations who wish to express the balance between Word and Table may want to arrange the interior space of their worshiping area in a way that expresses this balance. Many churches are finding that it is best to put both the pulpit and the Table in an off-center position to symbolize the balance between the two. The interior design of Bethel Presbyterian Church in Wheaton is an example of this. In this church, the pulpit is to the right of the congregation, and the Communion Table is to the left. But each is visible from all parts of the sanctuary. The design is such that they blend rather than clash. What I see when I worship in that church is an imagery of Word *and* Table working together harmoniously, rather than a picture of one element dominating the other.

I have also argued for congregational involvement in worship. I believe it is the function of space to foster rather than hinder congregational participation. Unfortunately, the typical Protestant church employs a very closed use of space. The aisles are often narrow and the pews are situated in a style similar to that of the lecture hall. This arrangement, combined with a dominant pulpit, doesn't inherently free the congregation for involvement in worship. There is very little space for musical processions, for artistic expression, for drama, or dance. When I am in this kind of space, I always feel that my natural inhibitions are being supported and a leader-dominated worship is being affirmed.

I'm attracted to the newer churches that have been built without pews in order to establish a degree of flexibility for different worshiping occasions and seasons of the church year. I asked Robert Taylor about the merit of this kind of arrangement. As an architect he advocates flexibility for the purpose of creating a sense of community. In an adaptable situation, a feeling of togetherness may be maintained whether the building is filled or only a small group has gathered. Simply rearrange the environment to ensure that the people sit close to each other.

Where space is used to enhance their relationship, people sustain each other. I feel more a part of the body of Christ in that place. But, when all I see is the back of someone's head, when there is no eye contact with other people, my sense of the unity of the body of Christ is impaired. In a semi-circle seating or a seating where two sides face each other, the sense of community is stronger. In my experience I have been edified and moved to deeper worship by observing the involvement of other people in worship. I have seen people communicate the joy of worship through their faces and gestures. For me, watching someone sing enthusiastically or prayerfully or humbly is a moving experience. By seeing others bow and kneel in prayer, or watching someone reverently receiving the bread and wine, my participation in the community action or worship is increased.

Dan Sharp captures my experience in these words: "I walk into one church and I'm moved to awe, reverence, and involvement. I walk into another, and I'm moved to talk and chatter." This is why I feel we need to create a space in our churches that inspires and helps us to worship.

Color

Since color is really part of the arts, a final word needs to be said about the use of color in the church. All of us are sensitive to color and have, through its various uses, applied certain meanings to color. For example, we associate red with blood, white with purity, gold with the sense of festivity, purple with dignity, green with growing, and dark colors such as dark blue, violet, or black, with despair and mourning.

Some thought needs to be given to the color of the

sanctuary itself. Jim Young, director of theatre at Wheaton College, feels that colors push him into specific psychological states. Referring to color in the sanctuary, he says, "Light frees you. . . . To experience a color which frustrates light keeps you from being free inside yourself to really worship." Furthermore, he says, "There is a need to have a neutral color. . . . When you put a color in [the sanctuary] through a banner, like the color of Pentecost red, it speaks loudly and clearly."

I am fascinated by the fact that the Christian church has ascribed religious meanings to particular colors and uses these colors during the seasons they represent. For example, during Advent the color of violet is used (or royal blue) to symbolize the posture of repentance and preparation the church makes for the coming of Christ. The festivity of Christmas is captured in either white or gold, while the green of Epiphany symbolizes continuity (as in the evergreen). Lent is of course the most penitential season of the church because believers during this period identify with Jesus' moving toward death. The identification with Christ's preparation for death is indicated by a deep violet which may change into black during Holy Week. Because Easter is a joyous festivity, the colors which communicate this sense of celebration are white or gold. Red, which depicts leadership and martyrdom, is used during Pentecost to signify the coming of the Spirit and the birth of the church, which in all ages, and even now in many countries is the martyred community.

I believe the use of color in the sanctuary is important because it helps create a mood. For example, I have learned to associate mood with the life of Christ in such a way that inappropriate colors now work against my worship. For example, I'm disturbed that some pastors wear black robes or even black suits in Sunday worship. Frequently, the gloomy, mournful black conflicts with the mood of the service. To see black, for example, on

Easter Sunday offends my sensitivity to the resurrection which calls for white, the color of festivity.

I realize some people argue that response to color is a learned response. However, advertisers recognize that colors do stimulate us on a subliminal level. And the meanings that the church has ascribed to violet, blue, white, green, red, and gold are universally recognized.

Color needs to be used in an appropriate way. Traditionally, the color of the season is found in a cloth placed on the Table and a hanging from the front of the pulpit. It must be remembered that color is the servant of the season and of worship. Its use should be underplayed and subtle.

One of the positive results of the communication's revolution of the twentieth century is the rediscovery of the arts as symbolic messengers. We are rediscovering the presentational nature of the arts. They express truth to us in an imaginative and pictorial way.

I am fascinated by the insights of modern psychology which suggest how important the symbolic life is to a healthy personality. Carl Jung has pointed out that the symbolic life best expresses the need of the human soul, while Karl Rogers reminds us that we live in the context of symbols—home, parents, touch, gifts, smile, handshake, flowers. These are symbols of our life in the world.

But the same principle is at work in the spiritual life of each Christian. Worship is a means through which we can see, hear, smell, taste, feel, and come into contact with the infinite. Therefore the arts can mediate the message of Christ and minister to me in the depth of my being. We Evangelicals are just now beginning to discover how God can meet us through the arts. The future of the arts in worship, I believe, holds considerable promise for us in our continued discovery of worship as a verb.

I am keenly aware that it is one thing to talk about worship renewal and another thing to actually experience it in the local church. We are dealing with sacred and holy ground when we attempt to bring about change in worship. Even if members of the congregation will admit the need to change the worship of the church, that change will not happen easily or quickly.

In some churches, present traditions are so sacred that many pastors will decide to preserve them, even if they believe change is needed. I have had more than one pastor confide that they longed for worship renewal, but they were afraid to suggest changes or implement new practices.

For some, the resistance to change may be rooted in satisfaction with things as they are. Many people simply like passive worship. They don't really care to become involved, to break through the mold of being a mere recipient. Others fear that change will get out of hand and that the character of the church will be threatened or altered by too much change.

My own impulse is to suggest that a church move slowly but deliberately into worship change. I've seen the disaster which can result from change that comes too suddenly. For example, in a church where I held a workshop that was attended by 20 percent of the congregation,

the pastor, enthusiastic about my suggestions, incorporated all the changes I suggested in a single Sunday. The
congregation, which had not been adequately prepared,
was caught off guard and rejected the changes out of
hand.

It is probably best to introduce change slowly after
prayerful study and discussion of the subject has taken
place. One church that I worked with declared its goal
and supported the pastor and leaders of the church as
co-participants in the process of becoming educated toward change.

If your church decides to adopt the fourfold approach
to worship (Preparation, Word, Table, Dismissal), you
may want to choose to work on only one part at a time.
For example, start with the Word. Establish a lay readers'
group to read Scripture, follow the lectionary, conclude
the readings with "Thanks be to God," include readings
from the Old Testament, the Psalms, the Epistles, and
the Gospels. Do this for a month or two or even a season
without making any other changes. Then, when the people have learned to want more Scripture, to enjoy the
reading of God's Word, and to listen with their hearts,
begin improvement in another area of your worship life.

Another good way to begin worship renewal is to adopt
the church year as the organizing principle of your worship themes. You may want to help people integrate their
personal and family devotions with the sacred year which
is organized around the life of Christ. Help them live
through the cycle of Advent, Christmas, and Epiphany
as a spiritual discipline. You may want to continue to
do the same with Lent, Holy Week, Easter, and Pentecost.
Or you may decide to let the second season, the cycle
of life, wait for another year.

It might be a good idea to develop a three- or five-
year plan for worship education and renewal in your
church. I cannot determine a plan for you. Each church
is different; consequently, each church must determine
its own agenda for the renewal of worship.

I'm fully aware that most of us have extremely busy and hectic schedules. And renewal in worship will take time and effort on the part of pastor and congregation. But the result of truly worshiping God is well worth it. God has called us to worship him, and worship him throughout all eternity is what we will do. Perhaps now is the best time to begin experiencing worship in the corporate community of our local church. Let's break through the passive mold of being observers or recipients. Let's become active participants and doers. Let's discover that WORSHIP IS A VERB.

Throughout *Worship Is a Verb* my concern has been to help you understand worship and to assist you in applying four principles of worship in your local church. It has probably already occurred to you that it is one thing to understand worship and to be open to worship renewal, and quite another thing to actually implement necessary changes.

I don't have to tell you that changes in worship are not easy to accomplish. Any kind of change is bound to produce a certain amount of friction, misunderstanding, and resistance among congregation members. There are always those who will resist changing the placement of a hymn, while others are ready to overhaul worship from beginning to end. Consequently, change in worship tests tempers and relationships. Pray, then, for God's grace, for patience, and for a willingness to be flexible.

The purpose of this guide is to provide you with pointed questions that will facilitate discussion and implementation of worship renewal. The questions and exercises in this guide are designed primarily for group study. Thus, I have included helpful suggestions for group leaders within each section in addition to the general suggestions at the beginning. But remember, the leader's responsibility is merely to *guide* discussion and *stimulate* interaction. He or she should never dominate a particular situation. Rather, the leader should *encourage* all members of the group to participate.

This guide does not intend, however, to tell you what to do. It is designed to give your study group some direction so that together you may discover what kinds of changes are desirable and appropriate for your church. As you study the biblical and historical sources of worship, you may decide to try one suggestion, but not another. Or, you may decide to make no changes whatsoever until the principles of worship have become more a part of your own experience. In any case, it is my intention not to impose a structure of worship on you, but to encourage you to interact with the ideas presented in this book so the changes you eventually make in your worship will reflect your understanding and experience.

I think it is also important for me to warn you against becoming discouraged. Many of us have neglected the study of worship for a long time, and we cannot expect to turn our worship around and become completely satisfied with our experience through a nine-week study. As I mention this, I am reminded of a comment made by a minister involved in worship renewal in his own church. "Worship," he said, "is an inexhaustible subject. When you can exhaust God, you can exhaust worship." His statement should be kept in mind by all who journey on the road toward worship renewal.

Worship renewal is a never-ending task that reaches into the mystery of God himself. Pray that God will lead you beyond a mere understanding of worship into the rich mystery of the experience of God himself and into his healing presence in your life.

SUGGESTIONS FOR THE STUDENT

To help you use this study most effectively, I suggest you follow a few simple rules. They can be classified under three headings: *Prepare, Participate,* and *Apply.*

Prepare:

1. Read the text, *Worship Is a Verb*, completely and carefully. Underline or highlight sections that you feel are important. Put a question mark next to those ideas or concepts you don't understand or with which you find it difficult to agree.
2. Answer each question thoughtfully and critically.
3. Do all your work prayerfully. Worship itself is prayer. As you increase your knowledge and skills in worship, do so in a spirit of prayerful openness before God.

Participate:

1. Don't be afraid to ask questions. Your questions may voice the questions of other members in the group. Your courage to speak out will give these people permission to talk and may encourage more stimulating discussion.
2. Don't hesitate to share your personal experiences. Abstract thinking has its place, but personal illustrations will help you and others remember the material much better.
3. Be open to others. Listen to other members' stories and respond to them in such a way that you do not invalidate their experiences.

Apply:

1. Commit yourself to be a more intentional worshiper. Involve yourself in what is happening around you.
2. Determine your gifts. Ask: What can I do in worship that will minister to the body of Christ? Then, offer your gifts and talents to worship.

SUGGESTIONS FOR THE LEADER

Like the worship that it advocates, this guide is dialogic in nature. Because this study has been developed around the principles of discussion and sharing, a monologue or lecture approach will not work. Here are several guidelines which will help you encourage discussion, facilitate learning, and implement the practice of worship.

1. Encourage the participants to prepare thoroughly and bring their Bible and their text, *Worship Is a Verb*, to class.
2. Begin each session with prayer. Since worship is a kind of prayer, learning about worship should be a prayerful experience.
3. Discuss each question individually. Ask for several answers and encourage people to react to the comments made by others.
4. Use a blackboard or an easel and paper. Draw charts and symbols that visually enhance the ideas being presented. Outline major concepts.
5. Always invite concrete, personal illustrations. For example, ask questions such as: Have you experienced that? Where? When? Describe how you felt in that particular situation.
6. Look for ways to practically apply the answers and suggestions offered. For example, ask: How would you include this in our worship? How would you feel about that change?

Following are suggestions, questions, and exercises for a nine-session study on worship. Much of the material presented, although helpful for the student, is written for the study group leader. Questions which the student should answer in preparation for each session, and which the leader can ask in the context of the group, appear in slanted type for emphasis.

SESSION ONE: WINDS OF CHANGE

Every church is made up of people who come from different traditions. Whenever I speak in either denominational or non-denominational churches, I find people who have been raised in a number of different Protestant traditions or even in the Catholic church. This is probably true of your church as well.

For that reason, it might be helpful to use this first session to explore the various worship traditions represented in your group. Use this as a time for sharing rather than as a study time. Allow this opportunity for all members of the group to relate stories and impressions concerning their corporate worship experiences—to get to know each other. Listen to each experience with interest and acceptance, even if someone's personal preference doesn't agree with yours. It is important for everyone to know that their feelings and experiences are significant and that their suggestions for worship renewal are worthy of serious consideration.

Here are some suggestions for initiating a discussion and keeping it lively and on target.

1. Find out what different worship traditions are represented in the class. Ask people to call out their backgrounds. Someone can list the various denominations on the blackboard and tabulate the number of people from each tradition.
2. Ask for a description of worship in each of the traditions. Allow time for interaction and discussion.
   How do you react to your early experiences today?
3. Encourage people to be honest about their worship backgrounds.
   Have you ever become dissatisfied with worship?
   Have you ever felt that you simply didn't worship?
   Why did you feel that way?
   What was happening in your worship?

4. In the first chapter, the author describes four concerns
   related to his worship experience:
   • "I began to see that much of our worship is domi-
   nated by the pastor."
   • "I began to feel that the congregation was little more
   than an audience."
   • "I began to sense that 'free worship' is not necessarily
   free."
   • "For me, the mystery was gone."
   Have you ever had similar experiences? Describe them.
5. The author mentions five new insights that he gained:
   • "I began to see that the primary work of the church
   is worship."
   • "I rediscovered that worship is a source for spiritual
   renewal."
   • "Worship became an active experience for me."
   • "I experienced a better balance between the Word
   of God and the Table of the Lord."
   • "I experienced a return of the arts to worship."
   *Looking back at your personal experiences, how do you react
   to the author's insights?*

SESSION TWO: WORSHIP CELEBRATES CHRIST

In the first session we concentrated on an examination
of our personal experiences in worship. The goal of this
second session is to help us understand the experience
of the early Christian worshipers.

1. A major concern of chapter two is that contemporary
   worship has been reshaped, perhaps even distorted,
   by the influence of the secular age in which we live.
   To illustrate this point, list the following statements
   on the left side of the blackboard.
   Worship is turned into entertainment.
   Worship is overly intellectualized.
   Worship is overly sentimentalized.

Worship centers on the self.
Worship centers on a non-Christian event.

Now ask the class to give several examples for each statement. List their responses in a column to the right. Together, discuss how each example affects worship.

2. It has been argued that an antidote to the presence of secularism in the church is to recover the sense that worship is a festive celebration of Christ's life, death, and resurrection.

Would someone from the outside describe your church as a festive group of people?

Are the festive occasions of your church rooted in the Christ-event? Explain.

3. This chapter contends that early Christian worship was festive because it re-presented the life and death of Christ as the event which creates and sustains the church. In this regard, New Testament worship is similar to Jewish worship which represents the Exodus as the redemptive event of Israel. In order to understand this very significant biblical point better, do a comparative study of the Exodus-event and the Christ-event.

Study the following Scriptures:

THE EXODUS—EVENT	THE CHRIST—EVENT
• Israel came out of Egypt.	Matthew 2:13–15
• God led Israel into the desert with signs.	Matthew 3:16–17
• In the desert, Israel sinned by refusing to trust God for food.	Matthew 4:3–4
• In the desert, Israel tempted God, demanding signs of his love.	Matthew 4:5–7
• In the desert, Israel deserted God to worship the image of the golden calf.	Matthew 4:8–11
• Moses went up the mountain to receive God's commandments.	Matthew 5:1
• At Mt. Sinai God organized Israel into twelve tribes.	Matthew 10:2–4
• God entered into covenant with Is-	

rael. He ratified the covenant with
blood.   Hebrews 9:15
 • Israel was persecuted and op-
pressed.   Matthew 27:27–31
 • Israel became God's people, the sign
of his redemption.   1 Peter 2:9

4. Like Jewish worship, Christian worship is rooted in an
event which it celebrates. This event and its power
to change our lives is communicated to us today
through a dramatic retelling and reenactment. Compare Nehemiah 6 with Acts 2 and Exodus 12 with Matthew 26:26.
 *Is there an underlying drama revealed in the worship of your
 church?*
 *Does your church think of the proclamation of the Word as
 a dramatic retelling of God's spoken Word?*
 *Does your church view the Lord's Supper as a dramatic re-
 enactment of the Christ-event?*
5. Let's test a partial definition of worship: "Worship tells
and acts out the Christ-event."
 Examine the worship service of your church.
 *Identify the ways in which the retelling and acting out of the
 Christ-event are occurring—in the order of worship, in
 preaching and the Lord's Supper, and in prayers, hymns,
 faith confessions, and anthems.*

SESSION THREE: THE ORDER OF WORSHIP

The specific purpose of this session is to apply the first
principle of worship (Worship celebrates Christ) to the
actual order of worship in the church. The concern is
that if worship celebrates Christ, then the actual order
of worship itself should tell and act out the life, death,
and resurrection of Christ. Hand a church bulletin out
to everyone in the group, then wrestle with the following
questions.

1. A good way to begin a discussion on the order of worship is to (a) write the phrase: "Worship celebrates Christ" on the blackboard, then (b) take a recent church bulletin and examine your current order of worship. It's probably best not to try to go into detail at this time. Rather, simply attempt to discover a story line in the order of your present worship service.

   How does the story of God's revealing and redeeming unfold in the sequence of your church's worship?

   What kind of spiritual experience does this order convey to the participants in worship?

   Now that you have looked at the general order of worship, examine more closely each of the four commonly accepted parts of worship: Preparation, Word, Communion Table, and Dismissal.

2. Have a group member list the six parts of Preparation on the board.

   In your own words, state the purpose of Preparation.

   How does your church currently accomplish that purpose?

   Would you describe your church as formal or informal? High or low?

   How can Preparation for worship be improved in your church?

3. Evaluate the place of the reading and preaching of the Word in the worship of your church. As we have seen, the biblical pattern is that of Word followed by response: God speaks; we respond. Look again at the order of worship in your bulletin.

   In what ways is the pattern of divine initiative and human response evident in the current services of your church?

   What is your reaction to the amount of Scripture read in the service of your church? Should it be increased? Decreased? State reasons for your answers.

   Should sermons be longer? Shorter? Explain.

   How can response to Scripture be improved in your church?

   Discuss why you think your church should or should not use the ancient kiss of peace?

4. Examine more closely the fourfold symbolic action at the Communion Table: He took, he blessed, he broke, he gave.

How are these four parts of Communion manifested in your present form of worship?

Do you think your church should attempt to make each of these parts of Communion more obvious? Why or why not?

How would you describe the experience of the believer in each part of Communion?

Should your church celebrate Communion more frequently? Less frequently? Give reasons for your answer.

5. The final phase of worship is that of being sent forth: benediction, order to leave, and recessional hymn.

In what way does the Dismissal in your church accomplish the sending forth?

When do you think it is appropriate for announcements to be read?

How could the sense of the joy and triumph of the Dismissal be magnified?

6. There is one more matter you may wish to address. In this session discussion has revolved around the external order of worship. A word of caution is needed. It is always easy when discussing the external order of worship to unintentionally neglect the inner experience. Review each of the four parts of worship.

Describe your inner feelings and experiences as you move through your present order of worship.

What changes would make this a richer personal experience?

SESSION FOUR: GOD SPEAKS AND ACTS

The purpose of this study is to emphasize the divine aspect of worship. All too often we look only at the human side of worship. We become more concerned about what we are doing than what God is doing in worship. We worry about our response and ask ourselves: Did I sing heartily enough? Did I listen with appropriate attention? Did I let the message speak to my heart? While these are all important concerns, we must not let our concentration on them cloud the fact that it is God who is speaking and acting through the signs of his presence.

1. Since this chapter emphasizes that God encounters us through signs, it might be a good idea to talk about the function of signs in general.
   What are some signs and symbols that are used by our modern society?
   What do these say about us as a people?
   What kinds of signs and symbols do you use to convey messages in your home?
   How does body language nonverbally communicate a person's feelings and thoughts?
2. Not only do human beings use signs to communicate to each other, but God also communicates to us through signs.
   Explain the following quotation from the text: "In worship there is a descending line established by God and an ascending line represented by my faith. And the intersecting point of these lines is the visible and tangible sign of God's grace."
   Once the existence of symbolic language in society has been established and carried a step further into God's means of communicating to his people, the study group will be ready to discuss more specifically the function of the Bible and the bread and wine as signs of God's presence and healing power.
3. Turn your attention to the Bible as a powerful sign of God's intention to communicate. While most Christians acknowledge that it is a record of God's communication in the past, sometimes they pay only lip service to the power of the Scriptures to communicate God's

Word in the present. Begin this discussion by looking again at the bulletin of your worship service.

How significant is the role that Scripture plays in the worship of your church?

How much Scripture is actually used in the various parts of your worship?

How do you feel about the following suggestions made by the author: "We must stop treating the Scripture reading as a preliminary," and "I urge that we start paying more attention to the way we read Scripture."

Explain why establishing a lay reader's group in your church should or should not be considered.

4. Initiate a discussion about how the Communion Table is a sign of God's presence and power.

How do you view the actions of eating the bread and drinking the wine? Do you see them as God's sign given to you? Or do you see them as signs of your faith to God?

How are these perceptions different?

Which of the four terms used to describe the Table of the Lord express most closely what you experience in your worship? Why?

5. Ask for personal experiences.

When and how did God actually communicate to you through the Scriptures in worship?

Have you ever experienced the inner healing of your emotions at the Table of the Lord? Describe your experience.

Session Five: Worship, an Act of Communication

This session deals with the application of the second principle of worship: *In worship God speaks and acts.* Therefore we want to approach this discussion considering those ways in which we may be sensitized to God's presence in our worship.

1. Begin by reviewing the means of communication given

to us by God—means which God himself uses to get through to us.

Give several examples from Scripture to illustrate how God has communicated to us in verbal, symbolic, and cultural ways.

Identify the symbolic and cultural kinds of communication which are occurring in the context of worship in your church.

How has God reached you through cultural forms of communication?

2. Next, examine ways to improve the communication of the primary symbols in worship—the Word and the Table. The text emphasizes the need to become more personally involved in the drama of worship.

List the author's four suggestions for improving communication of the meaning of the Word in worship.

Which of these are practiced in your present service?

What is your reaction to the idea of instituting those practices that are not currently part of your worship?

List the five suggested ways for improving communication of the meaning of the symbols at the Table.

Which of these are part of your present service?

How do you feel about changing your worship to include any or all of those practices not currently employed?

3. Generate specific ideas on how to improve communication through the secondary symbols of the Preparation and Dismissal. Encourage response to the following proposals.

What could be done at the beginning of your service to create an atmosphere that is more conducive to personal preparation for worship?

How could both the beginning and ending of worship more dramatically communicate that we are coming into his presence and that we are going into the world to serve?

Could your congregation be encouraged to adopt some more specific kinds of body language to portray outwardly what is happening inwardly? Give suggestions.

4. If worship is indeed a divine act of communication, then something will happen to those who are open to the work of the Spirit through worship.
Give some examples of how worship (a) evangelizes you, (b) educates you, (c) spiritually forms you.

SESSION SIX: WE RESPOND TO GOD AND EACH OTHER

The second principle emphasizes the divine aspects of worship, what God does in our midst when we come together. Now we turn to the human side of worship, to the dimension of response. Worship, as already mentioned, is a two-way communication. The pattern is first God acts, then we respond. In this session we want to look at the nature of our response, evaluate that response, and ask how we can improve it.

1. The text emphasizes the necessity of responding to God in all his power and majesty, and criticizes churches for lacking a sense of awe and mystery.
Describe the mood of your church. Would you characterize the dominant mood as one of awe and reverence? Explain.
Read Revelation 4 and 5. List some examples of awe found in this passage.
What examples of awe and reverence can you find in your hymns, prayers, responses, Scripture readings, Communion Table, and other elements of worship?
How can the worship of God in all his majesty and power be improved in your church?
2. In worship we not only respond to who God is, but also to what he has done, is doing, and will do. In Israel the worship of the people was a response to the Exodus. Now our worship is a response to the cross and the empty tomb.
In what sense do you feel the Holy Spirit moving in your congregation and initiating response?

The author describes his tendency to measure response in numbers. Explain how you measure response. What effect does your perception have on your worship?

Describe an inner response which you experienced recently in worship. Did this inner response express itself in any outward way? Describe.

3. We tend to decorate our surroundings for special events such as weddings, birthdays, and even funerals as an expression of the importance we attach to them. However, in many evangelical churches the use of ceremonial symbols in worship is suspect.

Why do you think this is so?

Are there certain services in your church when the ceremonial is used? What are they?

How do you respond to such a practice?

Have you been to worship services where you felt the use of decorations and symbols was too important, where it interfered with the Spirit and understanding of the congregation? Describe.

What kinds of ceremonials would you like to see added to or dropped from your present service?

4. The text, in suggesting that worship is a response to something specific, intends to emphasize the need to have a structure to guide and direct our response. The order of Preparation, the Word of God, the Table of the Lord, and Dismissal is a structure that tells a story and thus guides our response.

Look through your worship bulletin.

How does the order of your service encourage a response to what God has done, is doing, and will do?

How does the order of your worship guide you into an inner response to God?

How can the order of your service be improved so that the response is strengthened?

How does the order and freedom of your worship compare to the author's experience of freedom and order in the worship of the Plymouth Brethren Church?

In summary, we respond to God for who he is and what he has done. In developing the worship of a particular church, we need to account for this in the actual order of worship itself. For who God is and what he has done is expressed through the order of worship, the external form which evokes and assists our internal response. In the next session we look at more specific forms of response.

SESSION SEVEN: RETURN WORSHIP TO THE PEOPLE

In this session some specific suggestions about how to return worship to the people are made. Again, we will do well to remind ourselves that the responses to which we refer are not merely spontaneous responses drawn from mid-air. Rather, we are looking for specific ways to enter into dialogue with God through the order of worship which is already present. Perhaps the best approach is to make specific suggestions for each of the four parts of worship. You can then react to each.

1. In the Preparation a pensive atmosphere appropriate for dialogue is created.

   How do you prepare your heart for worship? Can you improve this practice? How?

   Do you think your service should begin with a procession? Who should march in?

   How do you feel about using the following ancient prayer salutation to introduce a prayer?

   Minister: The Lord be with you.
   People: And also with you.

   How can people become involved in the recognition of God, the confession of sin, and the words of forgiveness?

   Do you think the sequence of the Preparation should be memorized by all so that a conscious participation will occur?

How can variety be incorporated into this part of the service? Can it be handled through hymns? Psalms?

2. As mentioned, the pattern of worship includes reading and preaching the Word followed by appropriate response from the people.

> *How do you feel about adopting the ancient custom of responding in the following way at the conclusion of the reading of Scripture?*

> Reader: This is the Word of the Lord.
> People: Thanks be to God.

> *Can you think of other responses to the Scripture that would be appropriate and involving? What are they?*

> *Do you think Scripture should be read sometimes in dramatic form involving various members of the congregation to play particular parts?*

> *Is music, such as solos and choir anthems, a response to the Word or does it prepare people to hear the Word?*

> *How can a spontaneous response to the Word be incorporated into your service?*

> *Should the congregation recite the Apostles' Creed or the Nicene Creed as a response of faith to the Word?*

> *How can prayer be returned to the people? What do you think of the suggestions made in the text?*

> *Would you like to see the kiss of peace used in this church?*

3. Evaluate the response to the fourfold action which takes place during the service of the Communion Table.

> *An ancient custom still used in many churches today is the Sursum Corda (lift up your hearts). What do you think about using the following dialogue to begin the Lord's Supper?*

> Minister: The Lord be with you.
> People: And also with you.
> Minister: Lift up your hearts.
> People: We lift them up to the Lord.
> Minister: Give thanks unto the Lord.
> People: It is good to give him thanks and praise.

In the ancient church a brief prayer was said after the Sursum Corda *followed by the singing of the* Sanctus. *In this way the congregation was involved in a dialogue during the celebration of the Table. Here is the text of the* Sanctus *which is used in many churches today:*

Holy, Holy, Holy, Lord God of Hosts
Heaven and earth are full of your glory.
Glory be to thee, O Lord most high. .
Blessed is he who cometh in the name of the Lord,
Hosanna in the highest.

Do you think this text should be sung in the worship of this church?
The Lord's Prayer was often said by the entire congregation after the prayers of thanksgiving. Do you think the theology of presenting prayer to the Father when you are at the Table is appropriate? Explain.
Should the congregation sing hymns during the distribution of bread and wine? Why or why not? What kind of hymns would be most appropriate?
How would you feel about the laying on of hands for inner healing during the Communion? What other ways could the congregation minister to each other's needs during Communion?

4. The purpose of the Dismissal is to send us forth into the world to serve. Our whole walk is a response to God.

Do you think this is the most appropriate time to have the announcements?
Who should recess? The pastor alone? The pastor and the choir? The entire church? Give reasons for your answers.

Finally, as you think about response in worship, it might be a good idea to develop a service of worship which incorporates as many of these elements as possible. Try it sometime and see what kind of response you get.

SESSION EIGHT: ALL CREATION JOINS IN WORSHIP

It is easy for us to forget that God created all things for his glory. While we tend to spiritualize our Christian experience and set it apart from the material creation, the doctrines of creation and incarnation bring the faith back down to earth. All of creation is set to the praise of God, says the doctrine of creation. And the incarnation affirms this principle, for in the incarnation God the creator actually becomes his own creation. Through the womb of the Virgin Mary, God becomes present in and to his world. In sessions eight and nine we want to look at the implication of these central doctrines of faith.

1. Begin by probing for the various attitudes toward the use of material creation in worship held by study group members.

   Read Revelation 4:1–6. What does this passage say about the use of creation in worship?

   Read John 4:23. What does this passage say about the use of creation in worship? Compare this passage with the previous one.

   How do the theological doctrines of creation and incarnation relate to the above issue?

2. Take some time to discuss the meaning of each of the Christian seasons. List each season in a column on the left of the blackboard; then to the right add a column with the heading "The Meaning Of." To the right of that add a third column asking, "What can I do to enter its meaning?" With these three columns on the board, discuss the following questions and have a group member record the essential points of each response.

   What is the meaning of Advent?

   What spiritual discipline can I adopt during Advent which will help me enter into the meaning of Christ's life during this period?

   Repeat this sequence for each season.

3. Look at the way churches practice time.

Has the element of time been secularized in your church? How?

Would you like to see your church adopt the sacred calendar as a discipline of worship?

What elements of worship would your church jeopardize or lose by adopting the church calendar?

What would your church gain by following the sequence of the church calendar?

Would it be possible to integrate personal devotion, family devotion, and congregational worship into the church calendar year?

Relate a personal experience of passing through a season having adopted spiritual discipline.

What benefit could be derived if the entire congregation were committed to an integration of their spiritual journey with the church year?

Session Nine: Rediscover the Arts

The purpose of this session is to make some practical suggestions for the use of the arts in your church. Come to the session with your ideas in mind. If possible, bring specific examples and plan to describe what effect they may have on the other members of the congregation.

1. Music

Choose a hymn or musical number for each part of worship. State the mood it creates. How can it serve worship?

Suggest a hymn or musical number for each church season. How does each hymn evoke worship appropriate to the season?

2. Art

Bring an example of religious art to the session and suggest how it may assist the worshiper to praise God.

How could you specifically use art in the celebration of each of the sacred seasons?

Art may be expressed in the clothing worn by the minister.

Do you think the minister should wear some kind of vestment? What is your suggestion?

3. Drama

How would you turn Matthew 13:1–9 into a dramatic reading? How would you turn one of the following readings into a dramatic skit?

Advent: Matthew 1:18–23
Christmas: Luke 2:1–14
Epiphany: Matthew 3:1–17
Lent: Matthew 23:29–39
Holy Week: Matthew 26:30–55
Easter: Matthew 28:1–10
Pentecost: Acts 2:1–13

Can you suggest other readings that lend themselves to dramatic interpretation?

4. Dance

Where is the most appropriate place in worship to incorporate dance?

5. Color

Here are the appropriate colors for each season year. How do you suggest using them?

Advent . . . . .purple
Christmas . . . . .white
Epiphany . . . . . .green
Lent . . . . .purple
Easter . . . . .white
Pentecost . . . . .gold/white

6. Space

Examine the use of space in your church.
Does any single element, such as the pulpit or the Table, dominate the space in your church?
Is the seating of the people arranged for relationship or for one-way communication? Explain.
How would you change the use of space in this church? For what purpose?

RESOURCE BOOKS

Davies, J. G., ed. *Westminster Dictionary of Worship.* Philadelphia: Westminster Press, 1979. A must for every church library. Scholarly but highly readable articles on terms, denominations, symbols, etc.

Dix, Dom G. *The Shape of the Liturgy.* London: Dacre, 1945. A twentieth-century classic that initiated much of today's worship renewal.

Hustad, Donald P. *Jubilate! (Church Music in the Evangelical Tradition).* Carol Stream, Il.: Hope Publishing Co., 1981. Twenty-eight chapters cover the whole gamut of music—history, theology, order of worship, music and renewal, music and drama, congregational music, instrumental music, choirs, soloists. Comprehensive, scholarly, readable.

Webber, Robert. *Worship Old and New.* Grand Rapids, Mich.: Zondervan Publishing House, 1982. And up-to-date survey of biblical, historical, and theological data which will prove helpful to the pastoral staff and lay teachers of worship. Contains chapters on music, church year, architectural space, and a lectionary appendix, as well as a thorough bibliography.

RECENT TITLES FROM EVANGELICAL AUTHORS

Allen, Ronald B. and Gordon Borror. *Worship: Rediscovering the Missing Jewel.* Portland, Ore.: Multnomah Press, 1982.

Engle, Paul E. *Discovering the Fullness of Worship.* Philadelphia: Great Commission Publications, 1978.

Flynn, Leslie B. *Worship: Together We Celebrate.* Wheaton, Il.: Victor Books, 1983.

Howard, Thomas. *Evangelical Is Not Enough.* Nashville: Thomas Nelson Publishers, 1984.

Martin, Ralph P. *The Worship of God: Some Theological, Pastoral, and Practical Reflections.* Grand Rapids, Mich.: William B. Eerdmans Publishing Co., 1982.

Rayburn, Robert G. *O Come, Let Us Worship.* Grand Rapids, Mich.: Baker Book House, 1980.

Schaper, Robert. *In His Presence: Appreciating Your Worship Tradition.* Nashville: Thomas Nelson Publishers, 1984.

Webber, Robert. *In Heart and Home: A Women's Workbook On Worship.* Grand Rapids, Mich.: Zondervan Publishing House, 1985.